PRISM

READING AND WRITING Intro

Sabina Ostrowska
Kate Adams

with
Wendy Asplin
Christina Cavage

CAMBRIDGE
UNIVERSITY PRESS

CAMBRIDGE
UNIVERSITY PRESS

University Printing House, Cambridge CB2 8BS, United Kingdom

One Liberty Plaza, 20th Floor, New York, NY 10006, USA

477 Williamstown Road, Port Melbourne, VIC 3207, Australia

4843/24, 2nd Floor, Ansari Road, Daryaganj, Delhi – 110002, India

79 Anson Road, #06–04/06, Singapore 079906

Cambridge University Press is part of the University of Cambridge.

It furthers the University's mission by disseminating knowledge in the pursuit of education, learning and research at the highest international levels of excellence.

www.cambridge.org
Information on this title: www.cambridge.org/9781316624180

© Cambridge University Press 2017

First published 2017
20 19 18 17 16 15 14 13 12 11 10 9 8 7 6 5 4 3 2 1

Printed in Dubai by Oriental Press

A catalogue record for this publication is available from the British Library

ISBN 978-1-316- 62418-0 Student's Book Intro with Online Workbook Reading and Writing
ISBN 978-1-316- 62497-5 Teacher's Manual Intro Reading and Writing

CONTENTS

SCOPE AND SEQUENCE

UNIT	WATCH AND LISTEN	READINGS	READING SKILLS	LANGUAGE DEVELOPMENT	
1 PEOPLE _Academic Disciplines_ Communications / Sociology	Thai Fishermen	1: Profile of Jeremy Lin (personal profile) 2: A Very Tall Man! (book excerpt)	_Key Skill_ Previewing _Additional Skills_ Understanding key vocabulary Skimming Scanning to find information Reading for details Synthesizing	Family vocabulary Nouns and verbs • Singular and plural nouns	
2 CLIMATE _Academic Disciplines_ Geography / Meteorology	The Growing Ice Cap	1: The Coldest City in the World (article) 2: Cuba Weather (website)	_Key Skill_ Scanning to find information _Additional Skills_ Using your knowledge Understanding key vocabulary Reading for details Previewing Synthesizing	Nouns and adjectives Noun phrases	
3 LIFESTYLE _Academic Disciplines_ Anthropology / Education	Panama's Kuna People	1: Meet the Kombai (book review) 2: Student schedule (class schedule)	_Key Skill_ Annotating a text _Additional Skills_ Using your knowledge Understanding key vocabulary Previewing Scanning to find information Reading for main ideas Synthesizing	Collocations for free-time activities Vocabulary for study Time expressions	
4 PLACES _Academic Disciplines_ Geography / History	The Cenotes of Mexico	1: A World History of Maps (excerpts from a history book) 2: The Maldives: An Overview (fact file)	_Key Skill_ Reading for main ideas _Additional Skills_ Understanding key vocabulary Previewing Using your knowledge Annotating Scanning to find information Reading for details Synthesizing	Superlative adjectives Noun phrases with _of_ Vocabulary for places	

CRITICAL THINKING	GRAMMAR FOR WRITING	WRITING	ON CAMPUS
Analyzing and using a two-column chart	Subject pronouns The verb *be* Possessive adjectives	*Academic Writing Skill* Writing simple sentences *Rhetorical Mode* Descriptive *Writing Task* Write a profile of someone in your family. (sentences)	*Life Skill* Meeting people
Understanding and using a three-column chart	Prepositional phrases	*Academic Writing Skills* Capital letters Commas *Rhetorical Mode* Descriptive *Writing Task* Write about the weather in your city or town. (sentences)	*Life Skill* Using English measurements
Analyzing and organizing information	Parts of a sentence The simple present	*Academic Writing Skill* Main ideas and details *Rhetorical Mode* Descriptive *Writing Task* Write about the life of a student in your class. (sentences)	*Study Skill* Creating a test study plan
Classifying key words	*There is / There are* Articles	*Academic Writing Skill* Paragraph structure • Topic sentences *Rhetorical Mode* Descriptive *Writing Task* Write facts about your country. (paragraph)	*Life Skill* Places on campus

UNIT	WATCH AND LISTEN	READINGS	READING SKILLS	LANGUAGE DEVELOPMENT	
5 JOBS *Academic Disciplines* Business / Career Services	Utah's Bingham Mine	1: Find_my_job.com (web page) 2: Email chain about jobs (emails)	*Key Skill* Reading for details *Additional Skills* Using your knowledge Understanding key vocabulary Scanning to find information Reading for main ideas Synthesizing	Vocabulary for jobs Adjective phrases	
6 HOMES AND BUILDINGS *Academic Disciplines* Architecture / Engineering	To Build the Tallest	1: Architect's World: Expert Interview (article) 2: Skyscrapers (article)	*Key Skill* Predicting content using visuals *Additional Skills* Using your knowledge Understanding key vocabulary Scanning to find information Reading for main ideas Reading for details Synthesizing	Pronouns Vocabulary for buildings Adjectives	
7 FOOD AND CULTURE *Academic Disciplines* History / Sociology	Goat Cheese	1: Tea: A World History (article) 2: 10 of the Best by Cuisine (travel guide)	*Key Skill* Taking notes *Additional Skills* Using your knowledge Understanding key vocabulary Reading for main ideas Reading for details Scanning to find information Synthesizing	Vocabulary about food Count and noncount nouns	
8 TRANSPORTATION *Academic Disciplines* Engineering / Urban Planning	Modern Subways	1: Transportation survey (survey) 2: Transportation in Bangkok: Report (student report)	*Key Skill* Skimming *Additional Skills* Previewing Understanding key vocabulary Skimming Scanning to find information Reading for details Using your knowledge Reading for main ideas Synthesizing	Quantifiers Transportation collocations	

CRITICAL THINKING	GRAMMAR FOR WRITING	WRITING	ON CAMPUS
Using a Likert scale to evaluate and analyze	The pronoun *you* *Must* and *have to*	*Academic Writing Skills* Joining ideas with *and* • Simple sentences • Writing compound sentences with *and* Writing an email *Rhetorical Mode* Descriptive *Writing Task* Write an email about a job. (paragraph)	*Communication Skill* Writing emails to professors
Comparing and using data	Comparing quantities Comparative adjectives	*Academic Writing Skills* Compound sentences with *but* Supporting sentences *Rhetorical Mode* Comparative *Writing Task* Write a comparison of two buildings. (paragraph)	*Study Skill* College classes
Brainstorming Using idea maps	Subject-verb agreement Determiners: *a*, *an*, and *some*	*Academic Writing Skill* Concluding sentences *Rhetorical Mode* Descriptive *Writing Task* Write about a popular food in your country. (paragraph)	*Study Skill* Making notes in a text
Collecting data using questionnaires and surveys Analyzing data	Sentence word order: subject-verb-object Linking sentences with pronouns	*Academic Writing Skill* Giving reasons with *because* and results with *so* *Rhetorical Mode* Explanatory *Writing Task* Write a paragraph explaining the results of a survey about transportation. (paragraph)	*Life Skill* Getting to campus and around town

HOW *PRISM* WORKS

1 Video

Setting the context

Every unit begins with a video clip. Each video serves as a springboard for the unit and introduces the topic in an engaging way. The clips were carefully selected to pique students' interest and prepare them to explore the unit's topic in greater depth. As they work, students develop key skills in prediction, comprehension, and discussion.

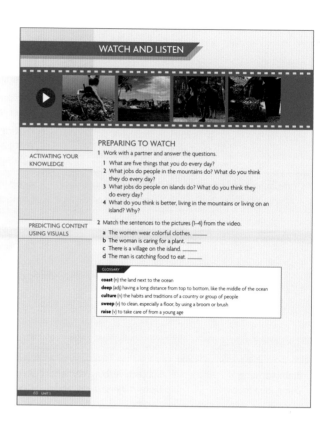

2 Reading

Receptive, language, and analytical skills

Students improve their reading abilities through a sequence of proven activities. They study key vocabulary to prepare them for each reading and to develop academic reading skills. A second reading leads into synthesis exercises that prepare students for college classrooms. Language Development sections teach vocabulary, collocations, and language structure.

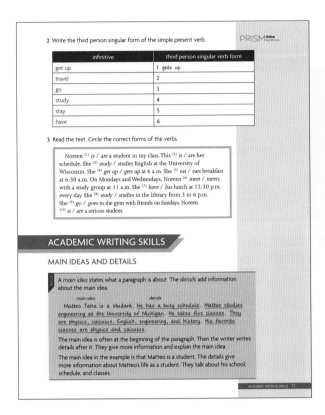

Critical thinking and production

Multiple critical thinking activities begin this section, preparing students for exercises that focus on grammar for writing and writing skills. All of these lead up to a structured writing task, in which students apply the skills and language they have developed over the course of the entire unit.

Skills for college life

This unique section teaches students valuable skills beyond academic reading and writing. From asking questions in class to participating in a study group and from conducting research to finding help, students learn how to navigate university life. The section begins with a context-setting reading and moves directly into active practice of the skill.

WHAT MAKES *PRISM* SPECIAL: CRITICAL THINKING

Bloom's Taxonomy

In order to truly prepare for college coursework, students need to develop a full range of thinking skills. *Prism* teaches explicit critical thinking skills in every unit of every level. These skills adhere to the taxonomy developed by Benjamin Bloom. By working within the taxonomy, we are able to ensure that your students learn both lower-order and higher-order thinking skills.

Critical thinking exercises are accompanied by icons indicating where the activities fall in Bloom's Taxonomy.

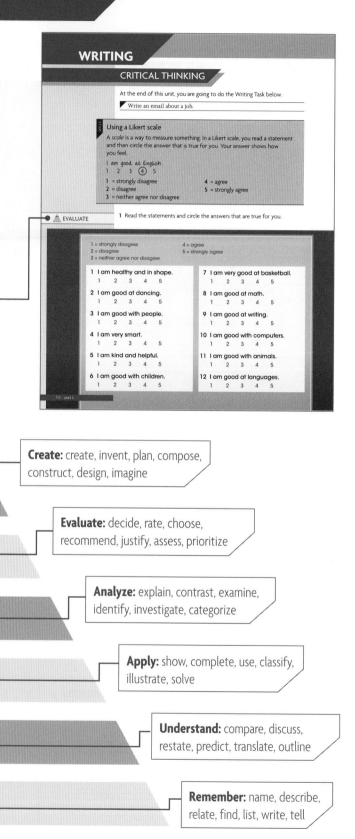

Create: create, invent, plan, compose, construct, design, imagine

Evaluate: decide, rate, choose, recommend, justify, assess, prioritize

Analyze: explain, contrast, examine, identify, investigate, categorize

Apply: show, complete, use, classify, illustrate, solve

Understand: compare, discuss, restate, predict, translate, outline

Remember: name, describe, relate, find, list, write, tell

WHAT MAKES *PRISM* SPECIAL: CRITICAL THINKING

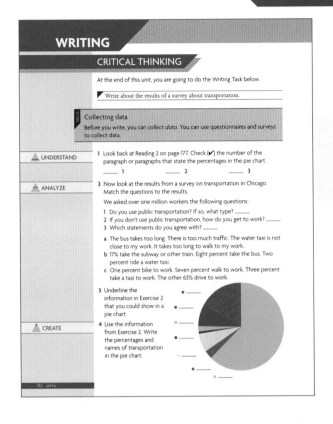

Higher-Order Thinking Skills

Create, **Evaluate**, and **Analyze** are critical skills for students in any college setting. Academic success depends on their abilities to derive knowledge from collected data, make educated judgments, and deliver insightful presentations. *Prism* helps students get there by creating activities such as categorizing information, comparing data, selecting the best solution to a problem, and developing arguments for a discussion or presentation.

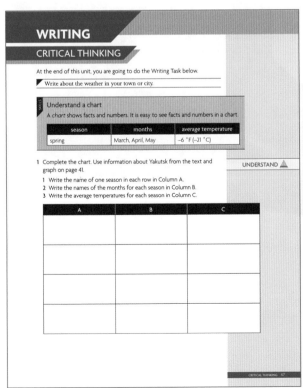

Lower-Order Thinking Skills

Apply, **Understand**, and **Remember** provide the foundation upon which all thinking occurs. Students need to be able to recall information, comprehend it, and see its use in new contexts. *Prism* develops these skills through exercises such as taking notes, mining notes for specific data, demonstrating comprehension, and distilling information from charts.

WHAT MAKES *PRISM* SPECIAL: ON CAMPUS

More college skills

Students need more than traditional academic skills. *Prism* teaches important skills for being engaged and successful all around campus, from emailing professors to navigating study groups.

Professors

Students learn how to take good lecture notes and how to communicate with professors and academic advisors.

Beyond the classroom

Skills include how to utilize campus resources, where to go for help, how to choose classes, and more.

Active learning

Students practice participating in class, in online discussion boards, and in study groups.

Texts

Learners become proficient at taking notes and annotating textbooks as well as conducting research online and in the library.

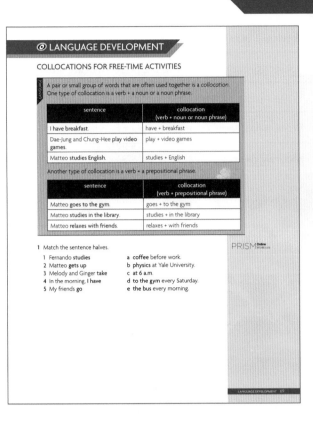

Vocabulary Research

Learning the right words

Students need to learn a wide range of general and academic vocabulary in order to be successful in college. *Prism* carefully selects the vocabulary that students study based on the General Service List, the Academic Word List, and the Cambridge English Corpus.

Grammar for Writing

Focused instruction

This unique feature teaches learners the exact grammar they will need for their writing task. With a focus on using grammar to accomplish rhetorical goals, these sections ensure that students learn the most useful grammar for their assignment.

LEARNING OBJECTIVES

Reading skill	Preview a text
Grammar	Subject pronouns; the verb *be*; possessive adjectives
Academic writing skill	Write simple sentences
Writing Task	Write a profile of someone in your family
On Campus	Meeting people

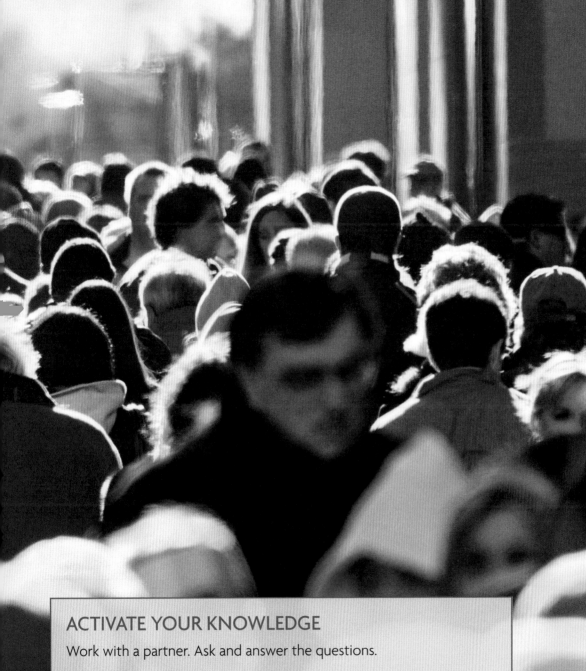

ACTIVATE YOUR KNOWLEDGE

Work with a partner. Ask and answer the questions.

1 What is your name?
2 Where do you live?
3 Do you have a job? What do you do?
4 Do you study? What do you study?

WATCH AND LISTEN

PREPARING TO WATCH

1 Work with a partner and answer the questions.

1 Where are you from?
2 What do you do in your free time?
3 Imagine you live by the sea. What could you do in your free time?

2 Look at the pictures from the video. Put the words in order to make sentences.

1 houses / There are / near the / water / .
2 The boys / a boat / on / are getting / .
3 in / are jumping / The boys / the water / .
4 the sea / in / He / is swimming / .

GLOSSARY

island (n) an area of land that has water around it, like Cuba or Iceland

spend time (v phr) to do something with your time

sail (v) to travel in a boat

dive (v) to jump into water with your head first

equipment (n) the things that you use for a particular activity

goggles (n) special glasses for seeing underwater

easily (adv) with no difficulty

WHILE WATCHING

3 ▶ Watch the video. Check (✔) the statements you hear.

1. ☐ Goon lives by the sea.
2. ☐ The Moken people spend a lot of time in and on the sea.
3. ☐ Goon does not like sailing.
4. ☐ The boys are good swimmers.
5. ☐ The boys need goggles to swim.
6. ☐ They can see everything underwater easily.

UNDERSTANDING
MAIN IDEAS

4 ▶ Watch again. Complete the sentences with the correct words from the box.

| friends   equipment   jump   family   village |

1. His _____ is near the west coast of Thailand.
2. They don't use special _____ or goggles.
3. They _____ from their boat into the water.
4. Goon and his _____ are special.
5. He catches fish and other sea animals for his friends and _____ .

UNDERSTANDING
DETAILS

5 Circle the correct word.

1. The Moken people learn to swim when they are *children / adults*.
2. The Moken people eat a lot of *meat / fish*.
3. A *boat / car* is important in the village.
4. The Moken people see easily in the water because *they were born with special eyes / they learn how to see underwater*.

MAKING INFERENCES

DISCUSSION

6 Work with a partner and answer the questions.

1. Would you like to live in a village near the sea?
2. Do you like to sail, swim, or fish? Why or why not?
3. How is Goon's life similar to yours? How is it different?

READING

READING 1

PREPARING TO READ

Previewing a text

Previewing means looking at a text before you read it. When you preview a text, look at the text and think about these questions:

1 Are there photos?
2 What is in the photos?
3 What is the title of the text?
4 Where is the text from? (a book? a magazine? a web page?)

PREVIEWING

PRISM Online Workbook

UNDERSTANDING KEY VOCABULARY

1 Look at the photo and the text. Ask and answer the questions with a partner.

   1 Read the title. What is a profile?
   2 Where can you find profiles?
   3 Who do you think Jeremy Lin is?

2 You are going to read a profile of a famous basketball player. Read the words and examples in the box. Then write the bold words from the box in the sentences below.

words	examples
languages	Spanish, Urdu, Russian
city	New York City, Montreal
date of birth	May 4, 1998
country	United States, Mexico
job	teacher, doctor
hobbies	reading, playing the piano, running

1 London is a very big _____ in England. Many people live there.
2 I speak three _____ : Turkish, Arabic, and English.
3 Morocco is a _____ in North Africa. It is next to Algeria and Spain.
4 My _____ is July 7, 1997.
5 I have a great _____ . I am a teacher.
6 I have many _____ . I like running, reading, and playing the piano.

FriendFile

MY PROFILE
Jeremy Lin

My personal information

First name: Jeremy
Last name: Lin
Date of birth: August 23, 1988
City: Torrance, California
Country: United States
Languages: English, Mandarin
Job: Basketball player

1

Email: jeremy.lin@cup.org

2

Mother: Shirley
Father: Gie-Ming
Brothers: Josh and Joseph

3

Hobbies: playing the piano, playing video games
Other interests: helping young people
Education: Harvard University

4

I'm Jeremy Lin. My mother and father are from Taiwan. I speak two languages: English and Mandarin. I am a basketball player. I have played on many basketball teams in the United States. My brothers' names are Josh and Joseph. They like basketball, too. I also like playing the piano and playing video games.

WHILE READING

3 Read the text on page 19 quickly. Write the words from the box in the blank spaces in the text.

> Contact information   My hobbies and interests
> My family   My life

4 Read the text again. Circle the correct words to make true sentences.

1 Jeremy is from *Taiwan / the United States*.
2 Jeremy's brothers like *basketball / video games*.
3 Jeremy's hobbies are *playing the piano and video games / playing the piano and basketball*.
4 Helping young people is Jeremy's other *job / interest*.
5 Shirley is Jeremy's *sister / mother*.
6 Gie-Ming is Jeremy's *brother / father*.
7 Jeremy's email address is *cup@jeremy.lin / jeremy.lin@cup.org*.
8 He went to *Harvard University / Boston University*.

5 Read the summary and circle the correct words.

> Jeremy Lin is a ⁽¹⁾ *basketball player / teacher*. He is from ⁽²⁾ *Torrance, California, / Harvard University* in the United States. His date of birth is August 23, ⁽³⁾ *1988 / 1998*. He ⁽⁴⁾ *speaks / plays* English and Mandarin. He has two ⁽⁵⁾ *sisters / brothers*.

DISCUSSION

6 Work with a partner. Ask and answer the questions.

1 What is your date of birth?
2 Do you have any brothers or sisters?
3 What are your brothers' and sisters' names?
4 What languages do you speak?
5 What are your hobbies?

READING 2

PREPARING TO READ

PREVIEWING

1 Look at the text and photos on page 22. Then circle the correct answers.

1 The man in the photo is
   a at a store.   **b** in his home.   **c** in a park.

2 The text is about a
   a farm.   **b** basketball player.   **c** very tall man.

3 The text is from a
   a book.   **b** magazine.   **c** web page.

2 You are going to read an article about an unusual man. Read the sentences. Write the bold words next to the definitions below.

UNDERSTANDING
KEY VOCABULARY

PRISM Online Workbook

1 That is an **unusual** job! I have never heard of it.
2 My brother is a student at an English university. He **lives** in London.
3 My father is a teacher. He **works** in a school.
4 Andrea is **interested in** languages. She wants to learn Japanese.
5 I like to listen to **music**. I like the sound of the piano.
6 I **watch** TV at night. I watch basketball games and other sports.
7 On a **normal** day, I go to work. Then I come home and eat dinner with my family.
8 My **family** is big. I have a mother, a father, four sisters, and three brothers.

a _____ (n) a group of people related to each other, such as a mother, a father, and their children
b _____ (adj) usual, ordinary, and expected
c _____ (v) to have your home somewhere
d _____ (adj phr) wanting to learn more about something
e _____ (n) sounds that are made by playing instruments or singing
f _____ (adj) different and not usual; often in a way that is interesting or exciting
g _____ (v) to do a job, especially the job you do to get money
h _____ (v) to look at something for some time

Sultan Kösen is a tall man.

A VERY Tall Man!

1 Sultan Kösen is from Turkey. He **lives** in Mardin in Turkey. He lives with his **family**. Sultan lives with his mother, his three brothers, and his sister.

2 Sultan is a farmer[1]. His hobby is **watching** TV. He is **interested in music**. His height[2] is **unusual**. He is 8 feet 3 inches (251 cm) tall—that is very tall. Sultan is the tallest man in the world. His mother, brothers, and sister are **normal** height.

3 Sultan **works** on the farm. He has a tractor. His life is not easy. People look at him in the street. Normal clothes and shoes are too small. His clothes and shoes are very big.

4 Sultan speaks Turkish and English. He went to London, Paris, and Madrid in Europe in 2010. He went to New York, Chicago, and Los Angeles in the United States in 2011.

tractor

[1] **farmer** (n) someone who owns or works on a farm

[2] **height** (n) how tall or high something or someone is

WHILE READING

3 Read the text and circle the correct words in the profile below.

> ## PROFILE
>
> First name: (1) *Sultan / Kösen*
>
> Last name: (2) *Sultan / Kösen*
>
> Country: (3) *Turkey / the United States*
>
> City: (4) *Mardin / New York*
>
> Family: (5) *three sisters and one brother / one sister and three brothers*
>
> Hobby: (6) *watching TV / working on a farm*

4 Read the text again. Write the correct words from the text in the blanks.

1 Sultan Kösen _____ from Turkey.
2 He _____ in Mardin in Turkey.
3 He lives with his _____ .
4 Sultan _____ a farmer.
5 His hobby is _____ TV.
6 Sultan _____ Turkish and English.

DISCUSSION

5 Work with a partner. Use ideas from Reading 1 and Reading 2 to answer the following questions.

1 Sultan's life is not easy. Why?

_____

2 What is Jeremy interested in? What is Sultan interested in?

_____

3 What can you learn from a profile?

_____

4 Do you like reading profiles? Why?

_____

FAMILY VOCABULARY

1 Write the nouns from the box in the correct places in the chart below.

brother	daughter	grandfather	mother	uncle

family vocabulary	
male	female
1 _____	grandmother
father	4 _____
son	5 _____
2 _____	sister
3 _____	aunt

NOUNS AND VERBS

Words for people, places, or things are *nouns*. Words for states or actions are *verbs*. Sentences have nouns and verbs.

nouns: **Sultan** is a **farmer**. He lives in **Mardin**. He works on a **farm**.

verbs: Sultan **is** a farmer. He **lives** in Mardin. He **works** on a farm.

2 Read the sentences. Write the bold words in the correct columns in the chart.

1 Jeremy Lin's mother and father are from **Taiwan**.
2 Sultan Kösen **lives** on a farm.
3 Jeremy Lin's brothers like **basketball**.
4 Sultan Kösen **works** in Turkey.
5 He **is** interested in music.
6 Jeremy Lin **plays** the piano.
7 Sultan speaks two **languages**.

nouns	verbs

Singular and plural nouns

Nouns are *singular* or *plural*. Singular means one. Plural means more than one. For most nouns, add -s at the end of the singular form to make the plural form.

singular nouns: Ray has a **brother**. His brother is a **farmer**.

plural nouns: Fernando has two **brothers**. His brothers are **farmers**.

Some plural nouns have irregular forms:

man → men

woman → women

person → people

3 Read the sentences and circle the correct words.

1 My mother has four *sister / sisters*.
2 I have only one *aunt / aunts*.
3 I have a *grandfather / grandfathers* in Canada.
4 My grandmother has two *son / sons* in the United States.
5 She has five *brother / brothers*.

4 Read the sentences and write the words from the box in the blanks.

brothers city languages lives sister plays

1 Jeremy _____ basketball.
2 Erika is my _____ . She lives with me.
3 She speaks two _____ : Arabic and English.
4 I have a sister and three _____ .
5 My grandfather _____ in Istanbul.
6 Rio de Janeiro is a big _____ . My mother works there.

WRITING

CRITICAL THINKING

At the end of this unit, you are going to do the Writing Task below.

▶ Write a profile of someone in your family.

1 Work with a partner. Ask and answer the questions about Sultan from Reading 2 on page 22.

1 What is Sultan's last name? _____
2 Where does Sultan live? _____
3 Who is in Sultan's family? _____
4 What is Sultan's job? _____
5 What are Sultan's hobbies? _____
6 What languages does Sultan speak? _____

2 Think of someone in your family. Use the chart to write information about the person.

first name	
last name	
date of birth	
city	
country	
family	
job	
hobbies	
languages	

3 Work with a partner and use your chart. Ask and answer questions like the ones in Exercise 1 about the person in your family.

GRAMMAR FOR WRITING

SUBJECT PRONOUNS

LANGUAGE

Subject pronouns can replace nouns. Use subject pronouns before a verb.
Subject pronouns are: *I, you, he, she, it, we,* and *they*.

I am Min Lee. (Always use a capital letter for the pronoun *I*.)	**I** = Min Lee
You are my sister. Laura and I are sisters.	**You** = Laura
Thomas is 26. **He** is 26.	**He** = Thomas
Sarah is a student. **She** is a student.	**She** = Sarah
Busan is a city in South Korea. **It** is a big city.	**It** = Busan
Matt and I are brothers. **We** are brothers.	**We** = Matt and I
Mohammed and Yusuf, **you** are my friends. Mohammed, Yusuf, and I are friends.	**you** = Mohammed and Yusuf
Eduardo and Ana are from Colombia. **They** are from Colombia.	**They** = Eduardo and Ana

PRISM Online Workbook

1 Work with a partner. Write the words from the box in the correct places
   in the chart.

> aunts   brother   daughter   father   grandfather
> mother   sisters   sons   uncles

she	
he	
they	

2 Read the sentences and write the words from the box in the blanks.

> He   It   She   They

1 My sister is tall. _____ is 5 feet 7 inches (174 cm).
2 My aunts are Mexican. _____ are from Mexico City.
3 My uncle likes basketball. _____ plays every day.
4 Los Angeles is in California. _____ is a big city.

THE VERB *BE*

The verb *be* has three forms in the simple present: *am*, *is*, and *are*. After *I*, use *am*. After *you*, *we*, and *they*, use *are*. After *he*, *she*, and *it*, use *is*.

singular		
subject	***be***	
I	am	tall. a student.
You	are	
He She It	is	

plural		
subject	***be***	
We	are	from Turkey. students.
You		
They		

Use *not* after *am / is / are* to make negative statements.

We **are not** brothers.   I **am not** from Busan.   They **are not** farmers.

Contractions

Contractions are used in informal writing and in speaking.

singular	plural
I am → I'm	we are → we're
you are → you're	you are → you're
he is → he's	they are → they're
she is → she's	
it is → it's	

Negative contractions

singular	plural
I'm not	we **aren't** / we're **not**
you **aren't** / you're **not**	they **aren't** / they're **not**
he **isn't** / he's **not**	you **aren't** / you're **not**
she **isn't** / she's **not**	
it **isn't** / it's **not**	

3 Read paragraphs A and B and write *am*, *is*, or *are* in the blanks.

A

My name (1)_____ Khalid.
I (2)_____ from Al Ain. I (3)_____
19. Al Ain (4)_____ in the United
Arab Emirates. My brother's name
(5)_____ Faisal. He (6)_____ older.
He (7)_____ 26. My father's name
(8)_____ Ali.

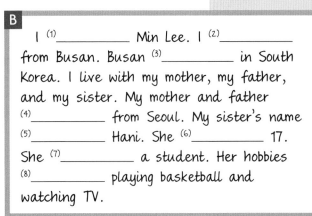

B

I (1)_____ Min Lee. I (2)_____
from Busan. Busan (3)_____ in South
Korea. I live with my mother, my father,
and my sister. My mother and father
(4)_____ from Seoul. My sister's name
(5)_____ Hani. She (6)_____ 17.
She (7)_____ a student. Her hobbies
(8)_____ playing basketball and
watching TV.

4 Write *am not*, *is not*, or *are not* in the blanks.

1 I _____ from Guangzhou. I am from Beijing.
2 Ana and Feride _____ sisters. They are friends.
3 Ahmed is from Jeddah. He _____ from Riyadh.
4 Daniella is from Brasilia. She _____ from Rio de Janeiro.
5 My parents _____ from China. They are from South Korea.
6 We _____ farmers. We are doctors.

POSSESSIVE ADJECTIVES

LANGUAGE

Possessive adjectives show that someone owns or has something. They can also show relationships. The possessive adjectives are: *my, your, his, her, its, our,* and *their*.

Use possessive adjectives before a noun.

subject pronoun	possessive adjective	
I	my	I am from Turkey. **My** city is Istanbul.
you	your	**You** are from Egypt. **Your** school is in Alexandria.
Natalia she	her	Natalia is from Italy. **Her** father is from Rome.
Sultan he	his	Sultan lives in Mardin. **His** family is in Turkey.
Japan it	its	Japan is in Asia. **Its** capital is Tokyo.
we	our	**We** have a big family. **Our** uncle is in Dubai.
Marta and Luis they	their	Marta and Luis have a sister. **Their** sister is a teacher.

PRISM Online Workbook

5 Read the sentences below and write the words from the box in the blanks.

Her His Its My Our Their

1 I have two sisters. _____ names are Frances and Celia.
2 Jenny Fielding is from Miami. _____ father's name is David.
3 We go to school in Los Angeles. _____ school is very big.
4 I have a brother and a sister. _____ sister's name is Andrea.
5 Jeremy Lin is from California. _____ mother is from Taiwan.
6 I live in a big city. _____ name is Montreal.

ACADEMIC WRITING SKILLS

WRITING SIMPLE SENTENCES

A *simple sentence* has a subject and a verb. The sentence is about the subject. The subject is a noun, noun phrase, or pronoun. The verb comes after the subject.

       subject verb
noun: Sultan is from Turkey.

             subject verb
noun phrase: His life is not easy.

        subject verb   *subject verb*
pronoun: I am from Beijing. **It** is a big city.

Begin the first word in a sentence with a capital letter (A, B, C). Put a period (.) at the end of the sentence.
He watches TV.

Remember: Sentences tell a complete thought. They always have a subject and a verb.

      subject   verb
✔ **Jeremy Lin plays basketball.**

    subject   missing verb
✗ **Jeremy Lin basketball.**

1 Put the words in order to make sentences.

  1 Zhong Shan / My grandfather's name / is / .

    _____

  2 is / He / 59 / .

    _____

  3 a doctor / He / is / .

    _____

  4 is from / He / Hong Kong / .

    _____

  5 two daughters / He / has / .

    _____

  6 my mother and father / lives with / He / .

    _____

2 Correct the mistakes in the simple sentences. Look for mistakes in capital letters and periods and a missing subject or verb.

1 my name is Gustavo

_____

2 i am from Ecuador

_____

3 i 19

_____

4 my father's name Marcus

_____

5 he a teacher

_____

6 he has two sons

_____

7 my brother's name is Paulo

_____

8 is a doctor

_____

9 he in Canada

_____

10 Paulo's hobbies playing the piano and watching TV

_____

WRITING TASK

Write a profile of someone in your family.

PLAN

1 Look back at your chart in Critical Thinking. Review your notes and add any new information you want to include in your profile. Think about:

- name
- date of birth
- city
- country

- languages
- job
- family
- hobbies

2 Refer to the Task Checklist as you prepare your profile.

WRITE A FIRST DRAFT

3 Write sentences about the person in your family. Use the words in the chart below and the information from your chart in Critical Thinking to help you.

A	B	C
My brother's name He His family His hobbies	is are	Luis. a teacher. from Bogotá. watching TV and playing basketball.
She He They We	live(s) with	my uncle. my mother and father.
	speak(s)	Portuguese. Spanish. Turkish. Korean. English. Arabic and English.

EDIT

4 Use the Task Checklist to edit your profile.

TASK CHECKLIST	✔
Make sure each sentence has a subject and a verb.	
Make sure each sentence begins with a capital letter and ends with a period.	
Use the subject pronouns *he* and *she* before the verb *is*.	
Use possessive adjectives (*my*, *his*, *her*) before a noun (*brother*, *sister*, *uncle*).	

5 Make any necessary changes to your profile.

ON CAMPUS

MEETING PEOPLE

Making friends

College students study a lot, but it is also important to have fun. Most colleges have clubs and special events for students, where they can make new friends and find new hobbies.

PREPARING TO READ

1 Work with a partner. Answer the questions below.

1 Do you like meeting new people?
2 Where do you meet new people?
3 What are your favorite hobbies?
4 Do you like sports? Which sports?

WHILE READING

2 Work with a partner. Read about college activities from three college students.

Mohammed

I am a member of the International Student Club. Members are from all over the world, like Mexico, Korea, and Turkey. Also, many members are Americans. It's a lot of fun. It's free. We have movies, dinners, and field trips together. Join a club!

Yumi

I am in a special night class. I take it for fun. It's Photography for Your Smart Phone. It's very interesting. The class is small. There are 12 students. The teacher is really nice. There are other classes, too. My friend is in an Indian cooking class! Take a fun class! Learn something new!

Min-jun

I like to play basketball. There is a team from my dorm. My English isn't good, but I can still play. There are nine guys on the team. We are all good friends now. It's exciting! Don't stay alone in your dorm. Play a sport!

3 Read the sentences and choose the correct words.

1 Yumi is in a _____ class.
   a travel   **b** photography   **c** cooking

2 There are people from _____ in the International Student Club.
   a the U.S.   **b** India   **c** the dorm

3 Min-jun likes to _____ .
   a speak English   **b** play basketball   **c** stay in his dorm

4 Yumi's teacher is _____ .
   a old   **b** nice   **c** international

4 Answer the questions.

1 Which activity is free? _____

2 Do you need good English to play basketball? _____

3 How many students are in Yumi's class? _____

PRACTICE

5 Read the activities brochure.

Welcome to the
Westside College Student Union.

Monday–Saturday
7 am–10 pm
Closed Sunday

There are activities for everyone. Come and meet new friends. It's fun!

GAMES (Student price: $6.00)	★ Bowling	★ Table Tennis
ART CLUBS (Free)	★ Dancing	★ Singing
LANGUAGE CLUBS (Free)	★ English Conversation	★ American Movies

6 Work with a partner. Circle two activities you like in the brochure. Which is your favorite one? Why?

7 Write about your favorite activities and clubs. Answer the questions.

1 Which activities and clubs do you like?

_____

2 Where are these activities and clubs on your campus?

_____

REAL-WORLD APPLICATION

8 Work in a small group. Go to the Student Union or activity center on campus.

1 Choose three activities or clubs on campus.
2 Ask these questions: What is the price? When is it open?
3 Make a brochure or poster for your favorite activities.
4 Share your brochure or poster with your class.

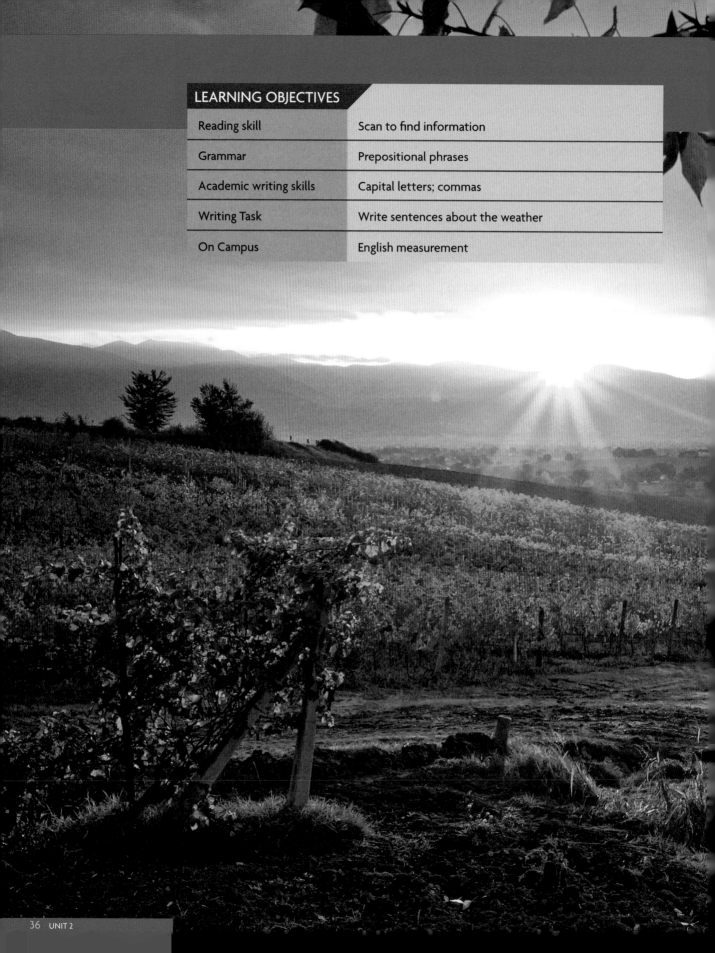

LEARNING OBJECTIVES

Reading skill	Scan to find information
Grammar	Prepositional phrases
Academic writing skills	Capital letters; commas
Writing Task	Write sentences about the weather
On Campus	English measurement

CLIMATE

ACTIVATE YOUR KNOWLEDGE

Work with a partner. Look at the photo and discuss the questions.

1 Does this look like a nice time of year? Why or why not?
2 Does this look like your country? Why or why not?
3 What time of year do you like best? Why?

PREPARING TO WATCH

1 Work with a partner and answer the questions.

    1 Which seasons do you have in your country?

    2 Do you prefer hot and sunny weather or cold and snowy weather? Why?

    3 Where in the world is it very cold?

2 Look at the pictures from the video. Write *T* (true) or *F* (false) next to the statements.

    _____ **1** This part of the Earth is warm.

    _____ **2** Part of the river is frozen.

    _____ **3** There is ice and snow on the trees.

    _____ **4** The trees die in the winter.

GLOSSARY

temperature (n) how hot or cold something is; for example, 32 °F or 0 °C

river (n) a long natural area of water that flows across the land

fir trees / pine trees (n) trees with thin, hard green leaves that stay green all winter

forest (n) a large area with many trees growing closely together

freezing / frozen (adj) very cold; turned into ice

heavy snow (n phr) a lot of snow

WHILE WATCHING

3 ▶ Watch the video. Check (✔) the statements you hear.

1 ☐ The days grow short and cold.
2 ☐ Winter is hard here.
3 ☐ Water in the air, in rivers, and in plants turns to ice.
4 ☐ All of the plants die.
5 ☐ Heavy snow covers the taiga.
6 ☐ Cold temperatures return in the spring.

4 ▶ Watch again. Circle the correct answer.

1 Snow and cold temperatures move *north* / *south*.
2 Fir trees can live in very *warm* / *cold* temperatures.
3 The taiga forest has almost *20%* / *30%* of all the trees on Earth.
4 Heavy *snow* / *rain* covers part of the taiga until the spring.

5 Complete the sentences with the words from the box.

difficult	flowers	near	winter

1 The _____ is very long in the taiga forest.
2 The taiga forest is _____ the North Pole.
3 Living in the taiga forest is _____ in the winter.
4 _____ do not grow in the winter in the taiga forest.

DISCUSSION

6 Work with a partner and answer the questions.

1 Do you think it is easy for people to live in the taiga forest? Why or why not?
2 How long do you think the winter is in the taiga forest?
3 Which season is the longest in your country?
4 What things do you take with you when you go to a cold place?

READING

PREPARING TO READ

UNDERSTANDING
KEY VOCABULARY

1 You are going to read an article about a city with cold weather. Look at the words in bold. Match the sentences.

1 California is **warm**.
2 Canada is **cold**.
3 **Spring** is before **summer**.

a In the winter, the temperatures are freezing.
b In the summer, everyone enjoys the sun.
c **Fall** is before **winter**.

2 Match the words to the correct numbers.

1 eleven   a 8
2 eighteen   b 18
3 twenty-one   c 6
4 forty-two   d 42
5 fifty   e 21
6 eight   f 11
7 six   g 50

USING YOUR
KNOWLEDGE

3 Look at the temperatures. Work with a partner and discuss the questions.

| 30 °F (–1 °C)   60 °F (16 °C)   80 °F (27 °C) |

1 Which temperature do you like best? Why?
2 What do people do outside for each temperature?
3 What are the temperatures where you live?

4 Look at the graph, photographs, and headings in the reading on the next page. Write *T* (true) or *F* (false) next to the statements.

_____ 1 Yakutsk is a city.
_____ 2 Winter is very cold in Yakutsk.
_____ 3 Summer is very cold in Yakutsk.
_____ 4 Svetlana has a café in Moscow.

The Coldest City in the World

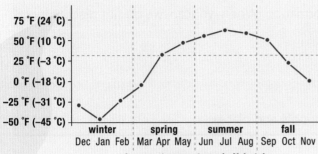

Average temperatures in Yakutsk
(December – November)

Ice skating

Skiing

1 The temperature in your freezer is **cold**. It is about 0 °F (−18 °C). The city of Yakutsk in Russia is colder than your freezer. In the **winter**, the average temperature[1] is −44 °F (−42 °C)!

2 In 2016, I visited Yakutsk. Why? Because I wanted to see the coldest city in the world. I wanted to meet the people of Yakutsk.

Svetlana has a warm café in a cold city.

3 "Life is difficult in the winter," says Svetlana, "but we're not sad." Svetlana is the manager of a café[2] in Yakutsk. She has two children. Her son Pavel is 11. Her daughter Daria is 5.

4 "The average temperature in the winter is −44 °F (−42 °C). Some winters are colder. At −40 °F (−40 °C), the kindergarten[3] is closed. Daria is happy. At −49 °F (−45 °C), the kindergarten and the school are closed. Daria and Pavel are happy," Svetlana says.

5 People in Yakutsk like sports[4]. In the **spring** and **fall**, the average temperature is −6 °F (−21 °C). They go skiing and ice skating. In the **summer**, it is **warm**. The average temperature is 68 °F (20 °C). People take food and drinks to eat outside.

[1]**average temperature** (n phr) how hot or cold a place usually is
[2]**café** (n) a small restaurant where you can buy drinks and food
[3]**kindergarten** (n) a class for young children, usually four or five years old
[4]**sports** (n) games or activities that people do to keep healthy or for fun

WHILE READING

Scanning to find information

Scanning means looking for information. When we scan, we do not read every word in a text. We can scan for:

- numbers
- names of people
- names of places

Look for capital letters to find people and places.

SCANNING TO FIND INFORMATION

PRISM Online Workbook

5 Match the facts to the correct numbers.

1	the average temperature in the summer	a −44 °F (−42 °C)
2	the year the writer went to Yakutsk	b 2016
3	the average temperature in the winter	c 5
4	Daria's age	d −49 °F (−45 °C)
5	the average temperature in spring and fall	e −6 °F (−21 °C)
6	the temperature when kindergartens and schools are closed	f 68 °F (20 °C)

READING FOR DETAILS

6 Write the words from the box in the blanks to summarize the text.

> cold   spring   Svetlana   warm   Yakutsk

> The text is about ⁽¹⁾_____ and her family. They live in the city of ⁽²⁾_____ in Russia. The winters are very ⁽³⁾_____ . Sometimes school is closed. In the ⁽⁴⁾_____ and fall, people go skiing and ice skating. In the summer, it is ⁽⁵⁾_____ .

DISCUSSION

7 Work with a partner. Ask and answer the questions.

1 Would you like life in Yakutsk? Why or why not?
2 When would you want to visit Yakutsk? Why?
3 How hot is the summer in your country?
4 What do you do in cold temperatures?

PREPARING TO READ

1 Work with a partner. Talk about the winter, spring, summer, and fall in your city or town. Do you have all four seasons? What months are in each season?

months	
January	July
February	August
March	September
April	October
May	November
June	December

2 Look at Texts A, B, and C on page 44. Circle the correct answers to the questions.

1 Where are the texts from?
   a a book   **b** a magazine   **c** a web page
2 Which text is about the weather in Cuba now?
   a Text A   **b** Text B   **c** Text C
3 Which texts are about typical weather in Cuba?
   a Texts A and B   **b** Texts B and C   **c** Texts A and C

3 You are going to read about the climate in Cuba. Read the definitions. Then write the words from the box in the blanks.

> **dry** (adj) with very little or no rain
> **rainfall** (n) the amount of rain that falls in one place
> **season** (n) one of the four periods of the year: winter, spring, summer, or fall
> **climate** (n) the weather that an area usually has

1 The _____ in spring is often high. It is good for the plants.
2 Summer is my favorite _____ . I like warm temperatures.
3 The desert is very _____ . Little rain falls there.
4 The _____ in the desert is hot and dry.

4 Write the words from the box in the blanks in Text B.

cloudy sunny rainy windy

CUBA WEATHER   HOME | WEATHER | CUBAN CLIMATE | WEATHER AVERAGE

1   Cuba is in the Caribbean. The **climate** in Cuba is good. It has two **seasons**: the **dry** season and the **rainy** season. The dry season and the rainy season each last for six months.
2   The dry season is from November to April. The average temperatures are between 72 °F (22 °C) and 77 °F (25 °C) in the dry season. The average **rainfall** is 2.6 inches (62 mm) in the dry season. It is **windy** and **sunny** in the dry season.
3   The rainy season is from May to October. In the rainy season, the average temperatures are between 79 °F (26 °C) and 82 °F (28 °C). The average rainfall in the rainy season is 5.7 inches (146 mm). It is often **cloudy**.
4   The best time to visit Cuba is April or May.

CUBA WEATHER   HOME | WEATHER | CUBAN CLIMATE | WEATHER AVERAGES

TODAY | TOMORROW | 5 DAY | MONTHLY

TODAY	MONDAY	TUESDAY	WEDNESDAY	THURSDAY
		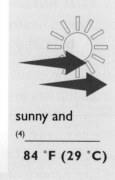		
(1)_____	cloudy and (2)_____	(3)_____ and cloudy	sunny and (4)_____	sunny
84 °F (29 °C)	82 °F (28 °C)	79 °F (26 °C)	84 °F (29 °C)	88 °F (31 °C)

CUBA WEATHER   HOME | WEATHER | CUBAN CLIMATE | WEATHER AVERAGES

SEASON (MONTHS)	AVERAGE TEMPERATURE	AVERAGE RAINFALL	AVERAGE WIND SPEED
Dry (Nov.–Apr.)	73 °F (23 °C)	2.6 inches (62 mm)	5 mph (8 kph)
Rainy (May–Oct.)	81 °F (27 °C)	5.7 inches (146 mm)	9 mph (15 kph)

WHILE READING

5 Read the three texts quickly. Match the facts to the correct numbers.

1 number of months in the dry season   **a** 79
2 average temperatures (°F) in the dry season   **b** 88
3 average rainfall (inches) in the dry season   **c** 73
4 average rainfall (inches) in the rainy season   **d** 5.7
5 temperature (°F) on Tuesday   **e** 6
6 temperature (°F) on Thursday   **f** 2.6

DISCUSSION

6 Work with a partner. Use ideas from Reading 1 and Reading 2 to answer the questions.

1 When is a good time to visit Cuba? Why do you think those months are good?
2 What are the seasons in Cuba?
3 Where can you find facts about the climate in a country?
4 Why do people want to know about the weather and climate of a place?

⊙ LANGUAGE DEVELOPMENT

NOUNS AND ADJECTIVES

> LANGUAGE
>
> Words for people, places, or things are *nouns*. Words that describe people, places, and things are *adjectives*. Adjectives can come after the verb *be*. They describe the subject.
>
> The winter is **cold**. The climate is **good**.
> August is **hot**. It is **cloudy**. It is **sunny**.

1 Underline the nouns and circle the adjectives in the sentences.

1 The café is warm.
2 October is rainy.
3 The climate is good.
4 Summers are hot.
5 Winters are cold.

PRISM Online Workbook

2 Read the sentences. Write the adjectives from the box in the blanks.

| cloudy cold difficult happy sunny |

1 In Yakutsk, life is _____ in the winter.
2 The children are _____ .
3 It is warm and _____ today.
4 The winter is _____ in Yakutsk.
5 The rainy season is _____ .

NOUN PHRASES

A *noun phrase* is a noun and another word that describes or defines the noun. When an adjective comes before a noun, it is part of a noun phrase.

noun phrases: Cuba has **a good climate**. Cuba has **a dry season**. **The average rainfall** is 2.6 inches. **The rainy season** is from May to October.

PRISM Online Workbook

3 Make a noun phrase from the bold words in each sentence. Write it in the blanks to make a new sentence.

1 Yakutsk's **winters** are **cold**.
Yakutsk has _____ _____ .
2 The **season** is **dry** from November to April.
The _____ _____ is from November to April.
3 In the rainy season, the **rainfall** is **high**.
The rainy season has _____ _____ .
4 **Summers** are **warm** in Yakutsk.
Yakutsk has _____ _____ .

4 Work with a partner. Correct the mistakes in the sentences. Look for mistakes in noun phrases or adjectives after the verb *be*.

1 Cuba has a season rainy.

_____

2 Yakutsk has a fall cold.

_____

3 In the summer, we have weather sunny.

_____

4 The dry season windy is.

_____

5 In spring, the rainfall high is.

_____

WRITING

CRITICAL THINKING

At the end of this unit, you are going to do the Writing Task below.

Write about the weather in your town or city.

SKILLS

Understand a chart

A *chart* shows facts and numbers. It is easy to see facts and numbers in a chart.

season	months	average temperature
spring	March, April, May	–6 °F (–21 °C)

1 Complete the chart. Use information about Yakutsk from the text and graph on page 41.

 UNDERSTAND

1 Write the name of one season in each row in Column A.
2 Write the names of the months for each season in Column B.
3 Write the average temperatures for each season in Column C.

A	B	C

2 Work with a partner. Look at the chart. Ask and answer the questions.

1 Is Yakutsk cold in February?
2 Is Yakutsk warm in August?
3 What is the weather like in April?
4 When is fall?
5 Is spring warm or cold?

 ANALYZE

3 Think of your own town or city. Circle the seasons there.

| dry season   fall   rainy season   spring   summer   winter |

 CREATE

4 Work with a partner. Create a chart for the seasons in your town or city. Use the Internet to find information.

season	months	average temperatures

PREPOSITIONAL PHRASES

The words *about, in, from, between,* and *for* are examples of *prepositions.* A *prepositional phrase* is a preposition + a noun. Use prepositional phrases to say where, when, how long, and to give an estimate or range.

where: Svetlana is **from Yakutsk.** Yakutsk is **in Russia.**

when: It is warm **in the summer.** It is cold **in January.**

how long: The rainy season lasts **for six months.** The rainy season lasts **from May to October.**

estimate or range: It is **about 0 °F (−18 °C).** The dry season lasts **about six months.** The average temperatures are **between 72 °F (22 °C) and 77 °F (25 °C).**

1 Read the sentences. Write the prepositions from the box in the blanks. You can use a word more than once.

PRISM Online Workbook

> about   between   for   in

1 People _____ Yakutsk like sports.
2 It is windy _____ the dry season in Cuba.
3 The average temperatures are _____ 79 °F (26 °C) and 82 °F (28 °C) in the dry season.
4 The temperature _____ your freezer is _____ 0 °F (−18 °C).
5 Winter lasts _____ three months in Yakutsk.

Prepositional phrases and punctuation

When a prepositional phrase begins a sentence, use a comma after it.

In the rainy season, the average temperatures are between 79 °F and 82 °F (28 °C).

In the spring and fall, the average temperature is −6 °F (−21 °C).

PRISM Online Workbook

2 Circle the prepositional phrase in the sentences.

1 In the dry season, the average temperatures are between 79 °F (26 °C) and 82 °F (28 °C).

2 The average temperatures are between 79 °F (26 °C) and 82 °F (28 °C) in the dry season.

3 Look at the sentences in Exercise 2. Answer the questions.

1 Which sentence has a comma after the prepositional phrase?

_____

2 What preposition is used to give a range in temperatures? _____

4 Write the prepositional phrases from the box in the blanks. Add commas if necessary.

in July   in the dry season   In the rainy season

1 It is warm in Cuba _____ .

2 _____ the average rainfall is 5.7 inches (146 mm).

3 The average rainfall is 2.6 inches (62 mm) _____ .

5 Put the words in order to make sentences. Place a comma if a prepositional phrase begins the sentence.

1 windy / October / , / is / it / In / .

_____

2 weather / good / the summer / is / The / in / .

_____

3 Cuba / climate / good / the / is / In / , / .

_____

4 the average / , / 1.3 inches (34 mm) / In the fall / rainfall / is / .

_____

5 Yakutsk / The / are / cold / winters / in / .

_____

6 / in / the summer / is / The average temperature / 68 °F (20 °C) / .

_____

7 the dry season / 2.6 inches (62 mm) / In / , / average rainfall / is / the / .

_____

PUNCTUATION

LANGUAGE

Capital letters

For the following types of words, the first letter is always a capital letter.

names of months: April, May, June

names of days: Monday, Tuesday, Wednesday

nationalities: Mexican, Egyptian, Korean

names of people: Juanna, Luis, Rodrigo

names of places: Turkey, Cairo, New York City

Commas

Commas separate parts of a sentence or things in a list. Use a comma:
- after a prepositional phrase at the beginning of a sentence
- when listing three or more items

In the winter, we go skiing.
In the summer, we go swimming.
It is going to be windy on Monday, Wednesday, Thursday, and Saturday.

1 Add commas to the items in the lists.

   1 It is spring in March April and May.

   2 It rains in spring summer and fall.

   3 The coldest months are December January and February.

   4 The warmest months are June July and August.

2 Correct the punctuation in the sentences. Add capital letters, commas, and periods.

   1 in january the weather is cold in Russia

   _____

   2 the average temperature is 70 °F (21 °C) in july

   _____

   3 in the rainy season the average rainfall is 5.7 inches (146 mm) in cuba

   _____

   4 the weather is sunny in the summer

   _____

PRISM Online Workbook

Write about the weather in your city or town.

PLAN

1 Look back at your chart in Critical Thinking. Review your notes and add any new information you want to include in your sentences.

2 Refer to the Task Checklist as you prepare your sentences.

WRITE A FIRST DRAFT

3 Write information about your city or town in the blanks below.

_____ (city or town) is in _____ (country).
_____ (city or town) has _____ (number) seasons.
The seasons are _____ .

4 Write sentences about your city.

1 Write a sentence about the weather in one season. (It is windy / cold / rainy.) Say which months the season is in (April / May).
2 Write a sentence about the average temperatures in this season.
3 Write a sentence about the weather in another season. (It is windy / cold / rainy.)
4 Write a sentence about the average temperatures in this season.

EDIT

5 Use the Task Checklist to edit your sentences.

TASK CHECKLIST	✔
Use adjectives before a noun or after the verb *be*.	
Use prepositional phrases to tell where, when, how long, or to give an estimate or range.	
Use commas after prepositional phrases that begin a sentence and for items in a list.	
Capitalize the beginning of a sentence and names of months, days, people, nationalities, and places.	

6 Make any necessary changes to your sentences.

USING ENGLISH MEASUREMENT

SKILLS

Measurement systems

There are two common measurement systems in the world. Most people use the metric system. People in the United States use the English system.

PREPARING TO READ

1 Work with a partner. Answer the questions below.

    1 Which of these measurements do you know?
    2 Which ones are easy to understand?
    3 Which ones are difficult?

> 75 °F   135 pounds   2.5 miles   a gallon of milk
> 6 feet 4 inches   an 8-ounce coffee   2 yards

WHILE READING

2 Read about the measurement systems in the United States and the rest of the world.

English measurement	metric measurement	how we use it	abbreviations & symbols
a gallon	3.8 liters	gas / milk	1 gal.
a quart	0.94 liters	milk / ice cream	1 qt.
an inch	2.54 centimeters	TV screen / pizza	54 in. / 12"
a foot	30.38 centimeters	people* / buildings	6 ft. / 85'
a mile	1.6 kilometers	trips	50 mi. long / 8,000 mi.
a pound	0.453 kilograms	cheese / fruit	2 lbs. / 3 pounds
an ounce	28.35 grams	coffee / soda	12 oz.

*Use feet and inches for people: 5 feet 4 inches, or 5' 4".

Most people measure temperature in degrees Celsius. People in the United States use degrees Fahrenheit.

3 Match the English measurement with the best metric measurement.

1 Three miles is about
  a three kilometers. **b** five kilometers. **c** six kilometers.

2 Two quarts is about
  a one liter. **b** two liters. **c** four liters.

3 6 feet 3 inches is about
  a 190cm. **b** 210cm. **c** 170cm.

4 Two pounds is about
  a one kilogram. **b** two kilograms. **c** four kilograms.

PRACTICE

4 Choose the right phrase from the box to complete the sentences.

1 gallon   21 years   85 miles   34 °F   5 feet 2 inches   16 ounces

1 Today it's (1)_____ outside. That's cold.

2 I have a nice cup of hot chocolate. It's (2)_____. It's a big cup.

3 I have a driver's license now. It says my age and my height.
  I'm (3)_____ old. I am (4)_____ tall.

4 My homestay family drinks (5)_____ of milk every day.

5 My dad drives me to school every day. He drives about (6)_____
  per hour. He drives very fast.

REAL-WORLD APPLICATION

5 In small groups, answer these questions using English measurements.
  Then ask two classmates.

	you	student 1	student 2
How far is your home from school?			
How tall are you?			
What is the temperature today?			
How much water do you drink every day?			

6 Visit a grocery store on your campus or in the neighborhood.

Find your favorite snack. What is the measurement? _____
Find a bottled drink. What is the measurement? _____
Did you see other measurement words or symbols in the store?
Write them here: _____

7 Report back to your class.

LEARNING OBJECTIVES

Reading skill	Annotate a text
Grammar	Parts of a sentence; the simple present
Academic writing skill	Main ideas and details
Writing Task	Write sentences about a student
On Campus	Create a test study plan

ACTIVATE YOUR KNOWLEDGE

1 Look at the photo and ask and answer the questions with a partner. Use the names of places from the box to help you.

café   library   park

1 Where are the people?
2 What are they doing?
3 Where do you study with friends? Why?
4 Where do you go with friends for fun? Why?

WATCH AND LISTEN

PREPARING TO WATCH

ACTIVATING YOUR
KNOWLEDGE

1 Work with a partner and answer the questions.

1 What are five things that you do every day?
2 What jobs do people in the mountains do? What do you think they do every day?
3 What jobs do people on islands do? What do you think they do every day?
4 What do you think is better, living in the mountains or living on an island? Why?

PREDICTING CONTENT
USING VISUALS

2 Match the sentences to the pictures (1–4) from the video.

a The women wear colorful clothes. _____
b The woman is caring for a plant. _____
c There is a village on the island. _____
d The man is catching food to eat. _____

> ### GLOSSARY
>
> **coast** (n) the land next to the ocean
>
> **deep** (adj) having a long distance from top to bottom, like the middle of the ocean
>
> **culture** (n) the habits and traditions of a country or group of people
>
> **sweep** (v) to clean, especially a floor, by using a broom or brush
>
> **raise** (v) to take care of from a young age

WHILE WATCHING

3 ▶ Watch the video. Check (✔) the statements you hear.

1 ☐ The Kuna people live in Venezuela.
2 ☐ Many of the Kuna are fishermen.
3 ☐ They also get food from their islands.
4 ☐ The Kuna always take care of their islands.
5 ☐ They work on big farms.
6 ☐ Music is important to Kuna men, women, and children.

UNDERSTANDING MAIN IDEAS

4 ▶ Watch again. Write *T* (true) or *F* (false) next to the statements. Correct the false statements.

_____ 1 About 35,000 Kuna men, women, and children live on islands near the coast of Colombia.
_____ 2 Kuna fishermen swim more than 200 feet deep.
_____ 3 They wear colorful clothes every day.
_____ 4 They have large gardens around their homes.
_____ 5 In their free time, they fish.

UNDERSTANDING DETAILS

5 Complete the sentences with the words or phrases in the box. You will not use all the words.

> colorful clothing   fish   land   long
> meat   music and dancing   short   swimming

1 The Kuna people have lived on the islands for a _____ time.
2 They often eat _____ .
3 They celebrate with _____ .
4 The Kuna people love and care for their _____ .

MAKING INFERENCES

DISCUSSION

6 Work with a partner and answer the questions.

1 Would you like to live on an island like the Kuna people do? Why or why not?
2 What are some good things about their lifestyle?
3 What are some bad things about their lifestyle?
4 How is their lifestyle different from yours?

READING

PREPARING TO READ

USING YOUR KNOWLEDGE

1 Ask and answer the questions with a partner.

1 Imagine you do not have a smartphone or TV. What do you do? How do you spend your time?
2 Imagine there are no supermarkets or restaurants. What do you eat?

2 Which things in the box can you see in the photos? Circle the words. Use a dictionary to help you.

> a writer   a hunter   a jungle   a tree house
> a TV   a website   a watch

UNDERSTANDING KEY VOCABULARY

3 You are going to read about a book that shows you a different way of life. Read the sentences and write each bold word next to the correct definition.

1 I do not like to wake up early. I **get up** around 10:00 a.m.
2 I like to **cook** my food at home, but many of my friends eat at restaurants.
3 Before I go to work, I have coffee and toast for **breakfast** every morning.
4 I usually eat **lunch** at my desk at work. I usually have a salad or soup.
5 I eat **dinner** after work. Sometimes, I eat with friends at a restaurant.
6 I often **travel** to China and Japan for my work.
7 I **meet** a lot of people in my job. I really enjoy talking with new people.
8 I **swim** every Saturday. I take lessons at a pool near my house.

a _____ (n) the food you eat at the end of the day
b _____ (phr v) to rise from bed after sleeping
c _____ (v) to see and speak to someone for the first time
d _____ (n) the food you eat in the morning after you wake up
e _____ (v) to move through water by moving your body
f _____ (v) to prepare food by heating it
g _____ (n) the food you eat in the middle of the day
h _____ (v) to go from one place to another, usually over a long distance

Meet the Kombai

Can you imagine your life with no smartphones or TV? With no cars or supermarkets? Can you imagine life in a tree house?

Kombai tree house

1   In her book, *A Life in the Trees*, journalist[1] Rebecca Moore **travels** 9,321 miles (15,000 km) from London to Papua New Guinea. In Papua New Guinea, Rebecca **meets** the Kombai people. She talks about their lives in the jungle.

2   Moore lived with the Kombai women and children for three months. Kombai life is very different. The Kombai people have no watches[2] and no cars. There is no school for the children. Parents[3] teach their children to **cook**, hunt, and **swim**.

3   The Kombai **get up** every morning at sunrise. Kombai men hunt in the jungle. They can hunt for 12 hours. They also cut down sago palms. This tree is important. The women cook the inside of the tree. The Kombai people eat this food for **breakfast**, **lunch**, and **dinner**.

4   The most important part of Kombai life is building their tree houses. The men, women, and children all help build tree houses. Each house is 66 feet (20 m) high. The stories in this book show the Kombai people's lives in the trees.

woman preparing the sago palm

Kombai hunter

[1]**journalist** (n) someone whose job is writing for newspapers
[2]**watches** (n) small clocks on a strap that you wear around your wrist
[3]**parents** (n) mother and father

WHILE READING

4 Read the text again and check (✔) the person or people that do each action. There may be more than one answer. The first one has been done as an example.

	Rebecca Moore	Kombai men	Kombai women	Kombai children
1 hunt in the jungle		✔		
2 travels 9,321 miles (15,000 km)				
3 cook sago palms				
4 eat sago palms				
5 have no cars				
6 teach children to hunt, cook, and swim				
7 build tree houses				
8 tells the story of the Kombai way of life				

5 Match the sentence halves to create complete sentences about the reading.

1 In Papua New Guinea, Rebecca meets
2 The Kombai women cook
3 The Kombai people have
4 The men, women, and children help

a the sago palm.
b the Kombai people.
c to build tree houses.
d a different life.

6 Read the text again to check your answers.

DISCUSSION

7 Work with a partner. Ask and answer the questions.

1 Why do you think the Kombai live in tree houses?
2 What do the Kombai people teach their children? Why?
3 What do you learn from your family? Why?

PREPARING TO READ

USING YOUR
KNOWLEDGE

1 List things you do on weekdays and on the weekend. Compare your list with a partner.

weekdays	weekend
Monday, Tuesday, Wednesday, Thursday, Friday	Saturday and Sunday

UNDERSTANDING
KEY VOCABULARY

PRISM Online
Workbook

2 You are going to read a college student's schedule. Read the sentences. Choose the best definition for the word in bold.

1 After lunch, I like to take a nap in the **afternoon**.
  a a time between 12 p.m. and 5 p.m.
  b something you eat for lunch

2 I am very **busy** with school. I take many classes.
  a having a lot of friends
  b having a lot of things to do

3 My **schedule** is the same every day. I work and then go to school.
  a a place where you work to make money
  b a list of planned activities or things that need to be done

4 I get up at 6 a.m. every **morning**. I make coffee and eat breakfast.
  a a time between 5 a.m. and 12 p.m.
  b the place where you make food

5 I **relax** after work. I watch TV.
  a to become calm and comfortable
  b to have many things to do

6 In the **evening**, I do my homework and read a book before bed.
  a a place you go to relax
  b a time between 5 p.m. and 11 p.m.

7 I have school on **weekdays**. I have to get up early.
  a Monday to Friday, when many people work
  b Saturday and Sunday, when many people do not work

8 On the **weekend**, I ride my bike. I have fun with friends.
  a Saturday and Sunday, when many people do not work
  b Monday to Friday, when many people work

3 Write the bold words from Exercise 2 in the correct places in the chart.

noun	verb	adjective	part of the day	part of the week

4 Look at the schedule and the text. Write *T* (true) or *F* (false) next to the statements.

_____ 1 The schedule is for an engineering student.
_____ 2 The schedule and the text are from a website.
_____ 3 The text and the schedule are about Matteo Taha.

Name of student: _Matteo Taha_   **Major:** _Engineering_

morning

	Sun.	Mon.	Tue.	Wed.	Thur.	Fri.	Sat.
8–9 a.m.		Physics 101	Physics 101	Physics 101	Physics 101	Physics 101	
9:15–10:15 a.m.		Calculus 121	Calculus 121	Calculus 121	Calculus 121	Calculus 121	
10:30–11:30 a.m.		Engineering 122	Engineering 122	Engineering 122	Engineering 122	Engineering 122	

afternoon

	Sun.	Mon.	Tue.	Wed.	Thur.	Fri.	Sat.
12:30–1:30 p.m.						Study group	
2–3 p.m.		English 101	Library	English 101	History 123		

evening

	Sun.	Mon.	Tue.	Wed.	Thur.	Fri.	Sat.
5–7 p.m.	Relax with friends	Library	Library	Library		Library	
7–10 p.m.	Relax with friends	Library		Go to the gym		Library	

Matteo Taha

1. Matteo Taha is a student. He has a **busy schedule**. Matteo studies engineering[1] at the University of Michigan. He takes five classes. They are physics[2], calculus[3], English, engineering, and history[4]. His favorite classes are physics and calculus.

2. Matteo has three classes every **weekday morning**. He gets up at 6 a.m. every day. Then he has physics from 8 a.m. to 9 a.m., calculus from 9:15 a.m. to 10:15 a.m., and engineering from 10:30 a.m. to 11:30 a.m.

3. On Monday and Wednesday **afternoons**, he has English. His English class is from 2 p.m. to 3 p.m. On Thursday afternoons, he has history from 2 p.m. to 3 p.m. On Friday afternoons, he meets with his study group. His study group is from 12:30 p.m. to 1:30 p.m. In the **evenings**, Matteo often studies in the library.

4. On the **weekends**, Matteo **relaxes** with friends. Sometimes, he goes to the pool to swim. He enjoys his busy life.

[1]**engineering** (n) the study of designing and building buildings, bridges, roads, etc.
[2]**physics** (n) the study of natural forces, such as energy, heat, light, etc.
[3]**calculus** (n) the study of a high level of math
[4]**history** (n) the study of past events

WHILE READING

Annotating a text

When you *annotate*, you mark the text. For example, you can underline key words. Key words are the words or phrases that give the important information in the text. Look at the underlined words in the paragraph below. The reader has underlined the key words that give the most important information and details.

> In her book, *A Life in the Trees*, journalist <u>Rebecca Moore</u> travels 9,321 miles (15,000 km) from London to Papua New Guinea. In Papua New Guinea, Rebecca <u>meets the Kombai people</u>. She tells about their <u>lives in the jungle</u>.

ANNOTATING

5 Read the text about Matteo again. Underline two to three key words or phrases in each paragraph. Then compare your key words with a partner. What is the important information?

6 Use the text and your key words. Circle the correct word to make true sentences.

1 Matteo has a busy *class / schedule*.
2 He is a *teacher / student* at the University of Michigan.
3 He takes five *classes / weekdays*.
4 He has three classes every weekday *morning / afternoon*.
5 He *relaxes / studies* on the weekends.

DISCUSSION

SYNTHESIZING

7 Work with a partner. Ask and answer the questions below.

1 When does Matteo relax? What does he do to relax?
2 When do you relax? What do you do to relax?
3 Use ideas from Reading 1 and Reading 2. Compare your life to the Kombai people and to Matteo. What is similar? What is different?

COLLOCATIONS FOR FREE-TIME ACTIVITIES

A pair or small group of words that are often used together is a *collocation*. One type of collocation is a verb + a noun or a noun phrase.

sentence	collocation (verb + noun or noun phrase)
I **have breakfast**.	have + breakfast
Dae-Jung and Chung-Hee **play video games**.	play + video games
Matteo **studies English**.	studies + English

Another type of collocation is a verb + a prepositional phrase.

sentence	collocation (verb + prepositional phrase)
Matteo **goes to the gym**.	goes + to the gym
Matteo **studies in the library**.	studies + in the library
Matteo **relaxes with friends**.	relaxes + with friends

PRISM Online Workbook

1 Match the sentence halves.

1 Fernando **studies**
2 Matteo **gets up**
3 Melody and Ginger **take**
4 In the morning, **I have**
5 My friends **go**

a **coffee** before work.
b **physics** at Yale University.
c **at 6 a.m.**
d **to the gym** every Saturday.
e **the bus** every morning.

2 Read the sentences and write the verbs from the box in the blanks.

| do   cooks   eats   go   have   meets   relax   take |

1 Matteo _____ **with** his study group on Fridays.
2 I _____ **a shower** before breakfast every morning.
3 You _____ **to the gym** every day.
4 Melody and Ginger _____ **breakfast** at 7 a.m!
5 Li Mei _____ **her lunch** in the café.
6 Sandra and Andreia _____ **with friends** in the evening.
7 My sister _____ **dinner** for my family.
8 You _____ **your homework** in the evening.

VOCABULARY FOR STUDY

PRISM Online Workbook

3 Read the names of the subjects. Check (✔) the correct box. Use a dictionary if needed.

subject	arts and humanities	business	math and science	language and writing
calculus			✔	
physics				
English composition				
economics				
biology				
history				
art and design				
chemistry				

4 Put the letters in the correct order to make the names of subjects.

1 alccsulu   c _____
2 snegihl   E _____
3 siphcsy   p _____
4 miechtyrs   c _____
5 ryshito   h _____
6 lobiogy   b _____
7 cmieoocns   e _____

TIME EXPRESSIONS

LANGUAGE

Time expressions say **when** or **how often** something happens. One type of time expression is *every* + a noun.

I do my homework **every week**. She has English class **every Wednesday afternoon**. They swim **every morning**.

Another type of time expression is a prepositional phrase for time. The preposition depends on the noun phrase that follows.

- *at* + clock time: **at** 10 a.m., **at** 3 p.m.
- *in* + part of the day: **in** the morning, **in** the afternoon, **in** the evening
- *on* + day of the week: **on** Monday, **on** Tuesdays
- *on* + day of the week + part of the day: **on** Monday morning, **on** Tuesday afternoon, **on** Friday evening, **on** Sunday night

PRISM Online Workbook

5 Write *at*, *in*, or *on* in the blanks.

1 Simon swims _____ Saturday morning _____ 8 a.m.
2 _____ the evening, Matteo studies in the library.
3 _____ Monday, I have English class _____ 2 p.m.
4 I talk to my family _____ the evening.
5 _____ Tuesday morning, David has calculus _____ 11 a.m.
6 Paulo goes to the university _____ Monday and Thursday.
7 I do my homework _____ the evening.
8 Andrea goes to work _____ 7 a.m. every day.

WRITING

CRITICAL THINKING

At the end of this unit, you are going to do the Writing Task below.

Write about the life of a student in your class.

UNDERSTAND

1 Work with a partner. Ask and answer the questions about Matteo. Look at the text on page 67 for help.

1 What is Matteo's last name? _____

2 What university does Matteo go to? _____

3 What classes does he take? _____

4 When does he get up? _____

5 When are his classes? _____

6 When does he meet with his study group? _____

7 When does he go to the library? _____

8 When does he relax with friends? _____

APPLY

2 Now talk with a partner about his or her life. Ask and answer questions like the ones from Exercise 1. Write your partner's answers in the schedule.

What classes do you take? When do you get up?

Name of student: **Major:**

morning

Times	Sun.	Mon.	Tue.	Wed.	Thur.	Fri.	Sat.

afternoon

Times	Sun.	Mon.	Tue.	Wed.	Thur.	Fri.	Sat.

evening

Times	Sun.	Mon.	Tue.	Wed.	Thur.	Fri.	Sat.

GRAMMAR FOR WRITING

PARTS OF A SENTENCE

Remember that a simple sentence has a subject and a verb.

subject   *verb*
The Kombai men hunt.

A simple sentence can also have an *object*, a *prepositional phrase*, or both.
An object is the person or thing that receives the action of a verb.

                    object
The women cook the food.

                        prepositional phrase   *prepositional phrase*
Rebecca Moore lived with the Kombai people for three months.

              object   *prepositional phrase*
They eat this food for breakfast.

PRISM**Online**
Workbook

1 Work with a partner. Match the sentences to the descriptions.

1 Matteo relaxes. _____
2 He has a busy schedule. _____
3 Matteo studies history at college. _____
4 The Kombai live in the jungle. _____

a subject + verb + object
b subject + verb
c subject + verb + prepositional phrase
d subject + verb+ object + prepositional phrase

GRAMMAR FOR WRITING 73

THE SIMPLE PRESENT

Use the *simple present* to talk about daily life.

I have breakfast every morning.

If the subject of the sentence is third person and singular, the verb ends with -s.

singular			plural		
subject	**verb**		**subject**	**verb**	
I You	swim	every day.	We You They	swim	every day.
He She It	swims	every day.			

To make the third person singular form (*he, she, it*) of a verb in the simple present, follow these spelling rules.

rule	third person singular verb form
Add -s if the verb ends in a consonant or a consonant sound.	cook → cooks live → lives
Add -es if the verb ends in -s, -z, -x, -ch, or -sh.	relax → relaxes watch → watches
Replace -y with -ies if the verb ends in a consonant + -y.	study → studies
Add -es if the verb ends in a vowel.	go → goes
Add -s if the verb ends in a vowel + -y.	say → says

Some verbs are irregular. Memorize their spellings. (have → has, be → is)

2 Write the third person singular form of the simple present verb.

infinitive	third person singular verb form
get up	1 gets up
travel	2
go	3
study	4
stay	5
have	6

3 Read the text. Circle the correct forms of the verbs.

Noreen (1) *is / are* a student in my class. This (2) *is / are* her schedule. She (3) *study / studies* English at the University of Wisconsin. She (4) *get up / gets up* at 6 a.m. She (5) *eat / eats* breakfast at 6:30 a.m. On Mondays and Wednesdays, Noreen (6) *meet / meets* with a study group at 11 a.m. She (7) *have / has* lunch at 12:30 p.m. every day. She (8) *study / studies* in the library from 3 to 6 p.m. She (9) *go / goes* to the gym with friends on Sundays. Noreen (10) *is / are* a serious student.

ACADEMIC WRITING SKILLS

MAIN IDEAS AND DETAILS

A *main idea* states what a paragraph is about. The *details* add information about the main idea.

       main idea   details

Matteo Taha is a student. He has a busy schedule. Matteo studies engineering at the University of Michigan. He takes five classes. They are physics, calculus, English, engineering, and history. His favorite classes are physics and calculus.

The main idea is often at the beginning of the paragraph. Then the writer writes details after it. They give more information and explain the main idea.

The main idea in the example is that Matteo is a student. The details give more information about Matteo's life as a student. They talk about his school, schedule, and classes.

PRISM Online Workbook

1 Read the paragraph. Circle the main idea and underline the details. Then answer the questions.

> Matteo has three classes every weekday morning. He gets up at 6 a.m. every day. Then he has physics from 8 a.m. to 9 a.m., calculus from 9:15 a.m. to 10:15 a.m., and engineering from 10:30 a.m. to 11:30 a.m.

1 What do the details say about …
   a Matteo's weekday mornings?
   b Matteo's engineering class?
   c Matteo's weekday afternoons?
2 What detail could the writer also include in this paragraph?
   a Matteo meets with his study group on Friday afternoon.
   b Matteo has breakfast at 7 a.m.
   c Matteo has English on Monday and Wednesday afternoon.

2 Read the paragraph. Circle the main idea and underline the details. Then add one more sentence to give another detail. Use your own ideas.

On the weekends, Matteo relaxes with friends. Sometimes, he goes to the pool to swim. _____
He enjoys his busy life.

WRITING TASK

PRISM Online Workbook

> Write about the life of a student in your class.

PLAN

1 Look back at the schedule you created for your partner in Critical Thinking. Review your notes and add any new information you want to include in your writing. Use it to plan the details for your sentences.

2 Refer to the Task Checklist as you prepare your sentences.

WRITE A FIRST DRAFT

3 Write answers in the blanks that are true for your partner.

_____ (*student's name*) is a student in my

_____ (*subject*) class. This is _____ (*his / her*) schedule.

4 Write sentences that are true about your partner's schedule.

1 Write a sentence about the subject(s) he / she studies.
2 Write a sentence about the time he / she gets up.
3 Write three sentences about his / her school or university schedule.
4 Write one sentence about his / her weekend or free time.

EDIT

5 Use the Task Checklist to edit your sentences.

TASK CHECKLIST	✔
Write a sentence that states the main idea.	
Write other sentences that add details.	
Spell simple present third person verbs correctly.	
Use the correct collocations for free-time activities.	
Use the correct prepositions for time expressions.	

6 Make any changes to your sentences.

ON CAMPUS

CREATING A TEST STUDY PLAN

SKILLS

Preparing for a test

In college, students often have to take different kinds of tests. For example:

- A **quiz** is a very short test. Some classes have a quiz every week.
- A **midterm exam** is a big test in the middle of the term.
- A **final exam** is a very important test at the end of the term.

Good students make test study plans on their calendars.

PREPARING TO READ

1 Work with a group and answer these questions.

    1 Do you have a lot of tests in your classes? What kind of tests do you have?

    2 How do you get ready for a test?

WHILE READING

2 Look at Rosa's test study plan for April.

MONTH: APRIL

Sunday	Monday	Tuesday	Wednesday	Thursday	Friday	
	1 Read my writing homework again	2 Meet my writing teacher	3 Midterm exam, Writing 1	4 Study new word list	5 Vocabulary quiz, Reading 1	6
7	8	9	10	11 Study new word list	12 Vocabulary quiz, Reading 1	13
14 Practice for speaking test with my study buddy	15 Speaking 2 test	16	17	18 Study new word list	19 Vocabulary quiz, Reading 1	2
21	22	23	24	25 Study new word list	26 Vocabulary quiz, Reading 1	2
28 Meet grammar study group 7pm	29 Review grammar book, chapters 1–2	30 Review grammar book, chapters 3–4	31 Midterm exam, Grammar			

3 Match the subject with the study task.

1 grammar	**a** study new word list
2 vocabulary	**b** meet with study group
3 speaking	**c** meet with teacher
4 writing	**d** practice with study buddy

PRACTICE

4 Write a new study plan for Rosa. Add study tasks for each test.

Sunday	Monday	Tuesday	Wednesday	Thursday	Friday	Saturday
	1	2	3 *Vocabulary midterm (word list 1–6)*	4	5 *Reading quiz (chapter 3)*	6
7	8 *Grammar quiz (simple present)*	9	10	11	12 *Writing midterm exam*	13

REAL-WORLD APPLICATION

5 With a partner, answer these questions.

1 What classes are you taking?
2 How many tests do you have this month?
3 Do you like to study with classmates? Why or why not?
4 How many days do you study for a test?
5 What other study tasks do you do?

6 Make a test schedule and study plan for the next month.

1 Choose a paper or phone calendar.
2 Write your test dates on the calendar.
3 Write study tasks for each test.
4 Show your plan to your group in class.
5 When you finish, put your study plan on your own calendar.

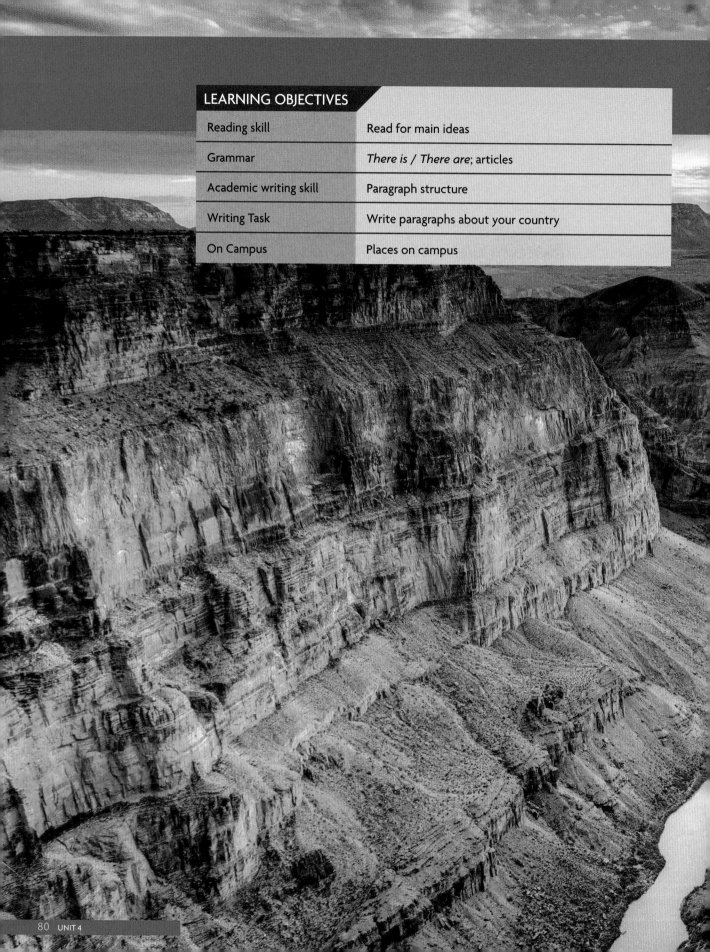

LEARNING OBJECTIVES

Reading skill	Read for main ideas
Grammar	*There is / There are*; articles
Academic writing skill	Paragraph structure
Writing Task	Write paragraphs about your country
On Campus	Places on campus

ACTIVATE YOUR KNOWLEDGE

Work with a partner. Ask and answer the questions.

1 What place is in the picture?
2 Why do people go there?
3 Do you want to visit this place? Why or why not?
4 What places do people visit in your country?

WATCH AND LISTEN

PREPARING TO WATCH

ACTIVATING YOUR
KNOWLEDGE

1 Work with a partner and answer the questions.

1 What makes a place special?
2 Why do people like to visit special places?
3 What special place would you like to visit? Why?

PREDICTING CONTENT
USING VISUALS

2 Look at the pictures from the video. Put the words in order to make sentences.

1 a monkey / There is / in the forest /.
2 in the trees / a space / There is /.
3 are growing / Plants / in the water /.
4 in the water / is swimming / A man /.

GLOSSARY

space (n) an empty area

full of (adj phr) containing a lot of things

lily pad (n) a large round leaf with a flower that floats on the surface of a lake or pond

turtle (n) an animal with four legs and a hard shell

WHILE WATCHING

3 ▶ Watch the video. Check (✔) the true statements.

1 ☐ There aren't many rich, green forests in the Yucatán.
2 ☐ The people in Mexico call the holes in the forests *cenotes*.
3 ☐ These holes are made of wood.
4 ☐ The scientist studies the trees there.
5 ☐ In the Yucatán, *cenotes* are the only places to find fresh water.
6 ☐ Most of the plants and animals live at the top of the *cenotes*.

4 ▶ Watch again. Fill in the blanks with the missing words.

1 These amazing holes are the only spaces in the _____ .
2 For Olmo, the *cenotes* are very _____ .
3 _____ is very important in the Yucatán.
4 *Cenotes* help the _____ and plants in the forest live.
5 When Olmo swims far into the cave, it gets _____ and dark.

5 Circle the correct word or phrase.

1 *Cenotes* are *very / not* important in the Yucatán.
2 Animals and plants *need / die in* the *cenotes*.
3 There *is / is no* life in the water.
4 It is *safe / dangerous* to swim far into the cave.

DISCUSSION

6 Work with a partner and answer the questions.

1 Are there any special places in your country like the *cenotes*?
What are they?
2 Would you like to visit the *cenotes*? Why or why not?
3 Would you like to swim in a cave? Why or why not?

READING

PREPARING TO READ

PREVIEWING

1 Look at the texts and the picture on page 85. Read the questions and circle the correct answers.

1 What is the book about?
   a the history of the world
   b the history of China
   c the history of maps
2 What is the first chapter of the book?
   a Discovering America
   b First maps of the world
   c Table of contents

3 What does the picture show?
   a a modern map of the world
   b an old map of the world
   c a photograph of the world

UNDERSTANDING KEY VOCABULARY

2 You are going to read a text from a history book. Read the sentences. Choose the best definition for the word or phrase in bold.

1 The Great Lakes in North America are very big, but the **lake** by my house is small.
   a salt water that covers most of the Earth
   b an area of fresh water that has land all around it
2 Lakes have fresh water, but **seas**, like the Mediterranean, have salt water.
   a a large area of very dry land
   b large areas of salt water
3 I do not like to climb **mountains**. I do not like to be up high.
   a very high hills
   b land that is low, near the water
4 There are many trees in a **forest**. They are homes for birds and other animals.
   a a large area of salt water
   b a large area of trees growing closely together
5 The Nile is the longest **river** in the world. It is 4,258 miles (6,853 km) long.
   a water that flows across the land to a bigger area of water
   b a large area of land with many trees
6 There are five **oceans**. These are the biggest bodies of water in the world.
   a one of the five main areas of salt water on the Earth
   b an area of sand or rocks next to water

7 People use **maps** to help them find places and understand an area.
   a pictures that show a place and the rivers, lakes, and other areas in it
   b boats, cars, and other things that people drive

Take a look!

A World History of Maps

by J. T. Kirk

Add to Basket

★★★★★

Price: from $16.75

Table of contents

A World History of Maps

by J. T. Kirk

Add to Basket

★★★★★

Price: from $16.75

2.2

Figure 2.3: World Map by Muhammad al-Idrisi, 1154

1   Muhammad al-Idrisi came from Morocco. He studied in North Africa and Spain. As a young man, he traveled in Spain, North Africa, France, England, and parts of Asia. In 1145, he began working for King Roger II of Sicily. Al-Idrisi created his **map** of the world then.

2   Al-Idrisi's map of the world is called the Tabula Rogeriana in Europe. The map is in Arabic. Al-Idrisi used information from earlier Arabic and Greek maps. He also used information from explorers. These men were sent to the different countries to draw and record what they saw. This map helped people travel from country to country.

3   The map shows North Africa, Europe, and South and East Asia. There are many European countries on the map. There is Norway in the north, Spain in the west, and Italy in the south. The map also shows India and China.

4   There are **forests**, **rivers**, **lakes**, **mountains**, **seas**, and **oceans** on the map. Al-Idrisi's map shows the Mediterranean Sea, the Indian Ocean, and the Nile River.

WHILE READING

3 Follow the directions to annotate the text about al-Idrisi's map.

1 Underline the name of a person important to the text in paragraph 1.
2 Underline the name of an important map in paragraph 2.
3 Underline the names of countries that the map shows in paragraph 3.
4 Underline the names of types of water the map shows in paragraph 4.

4 Scan the texts again and find the continents and countries that are mentioned. Circle them in the chart.

continents	countries
Asia	Finland
Australia	Spain
Europe	Norway
Africa	Canada
North America	Morocco
South America	China
Antarctica	The United States

5 Read Chapter 2.2. Write *T* (true) or *F* (false) next to the statements.

_____ 1 Muhammad al-Idrisi was Algerian.
_____ 2 The Tabula Rogeriana is written in Greek.
_____ 3 South America is not on the map.
_____ 4 India is on the map.
_____ 5 There are lakes on the map.

DISCUSSION

6 Work with a partner. Answer the questions.

1 How did al-Idrisi make his map?
2 What can you learn from a very old map?
3 How do you think maps are different today?

PREPARING TO READ

USING YOUR KNOWLEDGE

1 Ask and answer the questions with a partner.

1 What are important businesses in your country?
2 How many people do you think live in your country?
3 What is the climate in your country?
4 What languages do people speak in your country?

UNDERSTANDING KEY VOCABULARY

PRISM Online Workbook

2 You are going to read a fact file about an island country. Read the sentences. Write the words in bold next to the definitions.

1 Hawaii is a group of **islands** in the Pacific Ocean.
2 Mexico City is the **capital** of Mexico.
3 Many people enjoy the water and sun at the **beach**.
4 **Modern** cities have new buildings, parks, and businesses.
5 Arizona is **famous** because it has the Grand Canyon. Many people visit there.
6 **Tourists** visit the Grand Canyon because it is a beautiful place.
7 My school is **international**. There are students from all over the world.
8 Coffee with milk is **popular** in my country. Everyone drinks it. It's really good.

a _____ (n) a person who travels and visits places for fun
b _____ (adj) made with new ideas and designs
c _____ (n) land with water all around it
d _____ (n) an area of sand or rocks next to a sea, ocean, or lake
e _____ (n) the most important city in a country, where the government is
f _____ (adj) known by many people
g _____ (adj) liked by many people
h _____ (adj) relating to or involving two or more countries

The Maldives
– AN OVERVIEW

1 The Maldives are **islands** in the Indian Ocean. The islands are near Sri Lanka. The Maldives are **famous** for their good climate, beautiful **beaches**, and warm seas.

2 There are 370,000 people in the Maldives. Most people live on small islands.

3 The **capital** of the Maldives is Malé. It is a **modern** city with an **international** airport and a big harbor[3].

4 People in Malé speak English and Dhivehi. English is useful because many **tourists** come here.

5 Tourism and fishing are the most important businesses in the Maldives. There are many hotels. Many people work there. Others work as fishermen or in fish factories[4]. The currency is the rufiyaa.

[1]**currency** (n) the money a country or countries use
[2]**industry** (n) types of businesses
[3]**harbor** (n) area of water next to land where ships and boats can be safely kept
[4]**factories** (n) buildings where a large amount of things or products are made

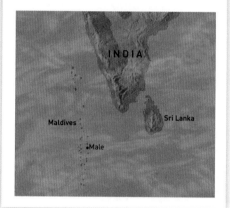

INDIA

Maldives

Sri Lanka

•Malé

One of the Maldives' beautiful beaches

MEET THE LOCALS

Ahmed Faiz, 19

6 I live on an island south of Malé. Life on my island is very simple. There are some stores, and there is one mosque. We speak Dhivehi, but we also learn English in high school. It is a nice place to live.

7 The Maldives are famous for their fish. There is a **popular** fish soup here. It is called *garudiya*. It is delicious.

8 People in the Maldives like to swim and dive.

Ahmed Faiz

WHILE READING

Reading for main ideas

Many texts have *paragraphs*. A paragraph is part of a long text. Each paragraph has a *topic* and a *main idea*. The topic is what the paragraph is about, for example, the weather. The main idea is the most important idea of the paragraph, for example, WHAT about the weather?

Tourism and fishing are the most important businesses in the Maldives. There are many tourist hotels. Many people work there. Others work as fishermen or in fish factories. The currency is the rufiyaa.

The topic here (what the paragraph is about) is tourism and fishing. The main idea (WHAT about tourism and fishing?) is that tourism and fishing are the most important businesses in the Maldives.

3 Read the text about the Maldives. Write the topics and the main ideas next to the paragraph numbers from the text.

READING FOR
MAIN IDEAS

PRISM Online Workbook

paragraph number	topic	main idea
1		
2		
3		
4		
5		
6		
7		
8		

DISCUSSION

4 Work with a partner. Ask and answer the questions.

SYNTHESIZING

1 Why do tourists go to the Maldives?
2 Do you want to visit the Maldives? Why or why not?
3 Use ideas from Reading 1 and Reading 2 to answer the questions: Why do people travel to different countries? What's important to know about a country?

SUPERLATIVE ADJECTIVES

LANGUAGE

Superlative adjectives describe how a person or thing in a group is different from all the others. Superlative adjectives have different forms.

Use *the* before a superlative adjective.

For one-syllable adjectives, add -*est*.
long → longest

The **longest** river is in Africa.

For one-syllable adjectives ending in -*e*, add -*st*.
blue → bluest

The **bluest** water is the Caribbean Sea.

For adjectives that end in one vowel + one consonant, double the consonant and add -*est*.
big → biggest   hot → hottest

The capital has **the biggest** population.

For adjectives with two or more syllables that end in -*y*, change *y* to *i* and add -*est*.
friendly → friendliest

The Maldives have **the friendliest** people.

For adjectives with two or more syllables, add *the most* before the adjective.
important → the most important   popular → the most popular

Tourism and fishing are **the most important** businesses in the Maldives.

The Maldives have many tourist sights, but the beaches are **the most popular**.

Some adjectives have irregular superlative forms.
good → the best

1 Rewrite the sentences using the superlative form of the adjectives in bold.

1 The Maldives have a **warm** climate.
   The Maldives have the warmest climate.

2 The Missouri River in the United States is **long**.
   _____

3 We live in a **big** city in Colombia.
   _____

4 The beaches in the Maldives are **beautiful**.
   _____

5 A **popular** dish in the Maldives is fish soup.
   _____

NOUN PHRASES WITH *OF*

One type of noun phrase is a noun + *of* + a noun.

Bogota is **the capital of Colombia**. Paris is in **the center of the country**. This book is about **the history of Japan**.

2 Match the sentence halves.

1 A world history	**a** of the United States.
2 The capital	**b** of Asia.
3 The dollar is the currency	**c** of Canada are English and French.
4 The main languages	**d** of maps.
5 Al-Idrisi's map shows parts	**e** of the Maldives is Malé.

VOCABULARY FOR PLACES

3 Write the words from the box in the correct places on the picture.

> beach   cliff   desert   farm   field   forest
> hill   mountains   sea   valley

WRITING

CRITICAL THINKING

At the end of this unit, you are going to do the Writing Task below.

> Write facts about your country.

SKILLS

Classifying

Classifying means putting words into groups with the same topic. Classifying helps you to plan your writing.

A writer brainstorms words to describe his or her country.

tourism   language   fishing   Dhivehi   industry   English

Then the writer classifies the words to organize and plan.

topic	key words
industry	tourism fishing
language	English Dhivehi

UNDERSTAND

1 Look at Reading 2 on page 88. Find the paragraphs with the topics in the chart. Then circle the key words that the writer used to discuss each topic.

topic	key words				
geography	islands	climate	food	Indian Ocean	near Sri Lanka
language	English	Thai	Dhivehi		
industry	tourism	fishing	cooking	currency	diving

APPLY

2 Find the paragraphs in Reading 2 with the topics in the chart. Then list the key words.

topic	key words
capital	
population	

3 Think about your country. Write five topics from the box in column A.

capital	climate	currency	food	geography
industry	language	population	sports	

A topic	B key words

4 Think of key words for the topics and write them in column B.

CREATE ▲

GRAMMAR FOR WRITING

THERE IS / THERE ARE

You can use *there is / there are* to say that something exists. Use *there is* before singular nouns and *there are* before plural nouns.

singular:

There is an airport in Malé.
There is a mosque on Ahmad Faiz's island.
There is a popular fish soup in the Maldives.

plural:

There are many countries on al–Idrisi's map.
There are many tourist resorts in the Maldives.
There are 370,000 people in the Maldives.

1 Put the words in order to make sentences.

1 are / in my country / different kinds / There / of businesses / .

_____

2 36 / languages / in Senegal / There / are / .

_____

3 modern airports / three / my city / are / in / There / .

_____

4 Seoul / There / of art / museum / in / a / is / big / .

_____

5 beach / beautiful / a / There / my / in / city / is / .

_____

2 Read the sentences. Check (✔) the correct sentences and cross out (✘) the incorrect sentences.

_____ 1 There are many languages in New York City.
_____ 2 There is mountains in Colorado.
_____ 3 There is many parks in San Francisco.
_____ 4 In Thailand, there are many islands.
_____ 5 There have many people in Buenos Aires.
_____ 6 There are many tourists in Quebec City.
_____ 7 They are many lakes in Michigan.
_____ 8 Is a big river in my city.

3 Correct the wrong sentences in Exercise 2.

_____
_____
_____
_____
_____

ARTICLES

Use *articles* before a noun or before an adjective + noun.

Indefinite articles (*a / an*)

A / An is the indefinite article. Use *a / an* with singular count nouns.

Use *a* before consonant sounds.
- *a river, a lake, a sea, a mountain*
- *a big river, a small lake, a cold sea, a tall mountain*

Use *an* before vowel sounds.
- *an ocean, an island, an hour*
- *an old city, an ancient map*

Definite article (*the*)

The is the definite article. Use *the* before the names of singular or plural places:
- rivers – *the Danube, the Nile, the Thames*
- seas – *the North Sea, the Mediterranean Sea, the Black Sea*
- oceans – *the Pacific Ocean, the Atlantic Ocean, the Indian Ocean*
- many famous places – *the Galata Tower, the Eiffel Tower, the Pyramids*
- "united" countries – *the United Arab Emirates, the United Kingdom, the United States of America*
- groups of islands – *the Antilles, the Azores*
- groups of mountains – *the Andes, the Alps, the Himalayas*
- plural countries – *the Philippines, the Maldives*

No article

Use no article before the names of:
- continents – *Asia, North America, Europe*
- most countries – *England, China, Turkey*
- cities – *Abu Dhabi, Bangkok, Shanghai*
- lakes – *Lake Superior, Lake Titicaca*

PRISM Online Workbook

4 Read the sentences and write *a, an, the,* or Ø (*no article*) in the blanks.

1 My family comes from _____ Chile.
2 _____ Chile is in _____ South America.
3 We live near _____ Pacific Ocean.
4 _____ Andes are the highest mountains in my country.
5 My sister lives in _____ United States.
6 She works in _____ Chicago. She lives near _____ Lake Michigan.

5 Correct the mistakes in the sentences.

1 I come from the India.

_____

2 Paris is an popular city with tourists.

_____

3 There is very tall building in Abu Dhabi.

_____

4 I go to an university in Boston.

_____

5 United Kingdom is in a Europe.

_____

6 I live by big lake.

_____

7 Ural Mountains are in Russia.

_____

ACADEMIC WRITING SKILLS

PARAGRAPH STRUCTURE

LANGUAGE

Paragraphs are groups of sentences that talk about one idea. This is called the *main idea*. Good paragraphs have three parts: a *topic sentence*, *supporting sentences* and *details*, and a *concluding sentence*.

The topic sentence usually comes first. The details, also called the supporting sentences, come next. The paragraph ends with a concluding sentence.

topic sentence	I live on an island south of Malé.		
supporting sentences / details	Life on my island is very simple.	There are some stores, and there is one mosque.	We speak Dhivehi, but we also learn English in high school.
concluding sentence	It is a nice place to live.		

Topic sentences

The topic sentence tells the reader what the paragraph is about. It tells the main idea of the paragraph. In the paragraph above, the topic is "an island south of Malé," and the main idea in the topic sentence is that it is where the writer lives. The topic sentence is usually the first sentence in a paragraph. Then the following sentences add details to the topic.

1 Read each group of sentences. Underline the topic sentence in each.

PRISM Online Workbook

1   The Maldives are islands in the Indian Ocean. The islands are near Sri Lanka. The Maldives are famous for their good climate, beautiful beaches, and warm seas.

2   Tourism and fishing are the most important businesses in the Maldives. There are many tourist resorts. Many people work there. Others work as fishermen or in fish factories. The currency is the rufiyaa.

2 Read each group of sentences. Choose the right topic sentence and compare with a partner.

1 There are many restaurants, and there is a public market. You can buy fresh fish, vegetables, and many other delicious food there. Everyone loves eating in Barcelona.
a Eating is an important part of visiting Barcelona.
b You can do many things in Barcelona.
c Barcelona is a city in the north of Spain.

2 The mountains are beautiful, but people also enjoy the forests and lakes in Canada. It's a popular tourist place.
a Toronto is the biggest city in Canada.
b Many people come to visit Canada every year.
c Canada is one of the largest countries in the world.

3 Read the sentences and write your own topic sentence. Then compare with a partner.

Many people live in the capital. There are lots of things to do and see. It is a busy and interesting place to live.

_____ .

WRITING TASK

Write facts about your country.

PLAN

1 Look back at the notes you created about your country in Critical Thinking. Choose three topics to write paragraphs about. Review the words and phrases you will use and add any new information you want to include in your writing.

2 Refer to the Task Checklist on page 99 as you prepare your paragraphs.

WRITE A FIRST DRAFT

3 Write a topic sentence and a supporting sentence for each topic. Use the key words to help you.

> The capital of my country is Bangkok. It is the most famous city in the country. There are more than 8 million people living there.

EDIT

4 Now use the Task Checklist to edit your paragraphs.

TASK CHECKLIST	✔
Write three short paragraphs.	
Write a topic sentence for each paragraph.	
Write 1–2 supporting sentences for each topic sentence.	
Use *there is* before singular nouns and *there are* before plural nouns.	
Use *the* before the names of rivers, seas, oceans, some countries, and famous places.	
Use no article before the names of continents, some countries, and cities.	

5 Make any necessary changes to your paragraphs.

ON CAMPUS

PLACES ON CAMPUS

SKILLS

Resources on campus

There are many resources on every campus. A resource is something you can use to help you. It can be a place, like a computer lab. It can also be a person, like a tutor.

PREPARING TO READ

1 Work with a partner and answer the questions.

    1 Do you ask people for help at your college? Who do you ask?

    2 What resources can you find on your campus?

WHILE READING

2 Read the three announcements from a college bulletin board.

3 Work with a partner. Complete the chart.

	library	bookstore	writing center
what?	tour	sale	workshop
when?			
where?			

FREE LIBRARY TOURS

Come on a library tour with a librarian.

Learn about our resources. We have books, journals, and online resources.

We are here to help you.

Tours are every Wednesday at 1 p.m.

Meet in Study Room A.

University Bookstore

SALE! March 4–11!

All dictionaries are 50% off! We can help you find the perfect dictionary.

For help, come to the Information Desk near the entrance.

This sale is for students only. Please bring your Student ID card.

New Writing Workshop[1]

Do you need help with your writing?

There is a new Writing Center in 401 Smith Hall! We have writing workshops every day.

We help all students.

Sign up online.

See you there!

[1] Workshop (n) a special class on one topic only

4 Answer the questions.

1 Who will give the library tour? _____

2 Where do students sign up for the Writing Center?
_____

3 What is on sale at the university bookstore? _____

4 Can your teacher get a 50% discount? _____

PRACTICE

5 Work with a partner. Complete each sentence with a word or phrase from the box.

> bookstore   library   writing center   international student services
> health center   housing office   tutoring center   transportation center

1 Melek has three classes. She studies hard, but her chemistry class is difficult. People at the _____ can help her.

2 Melek's writing homework is also very hard. The _____ is a good resource. They will help her a lot.

3 Melek wants to go to Canada, but she's not sure about her i20 and her visa. _____ can help her.

4 Melek has questions about the bus to the airport. There is a _____ in the Student Union.

5 Melek doesn't like her apartment. It is 20 miles from campus. Also, she wants a roommate. The _____ can help her.

6 Melek doesn't feel well. She wants to see a doctor. There is a _____ on campus. The doctors and nurses are very kind and helpful.

REAL-WORLD APPLICATION

6 Work with a small group. Which of the resources from Exercise 5 are on your campus? Choose two places to visit with your group.

7 Answer the questions for each place you visit.

1 Where is it?

2 When is it open?

3 What do they do? How do they help students?

8 Make an information sheet and report the findings to your class. Use the notices from the reading as examples.

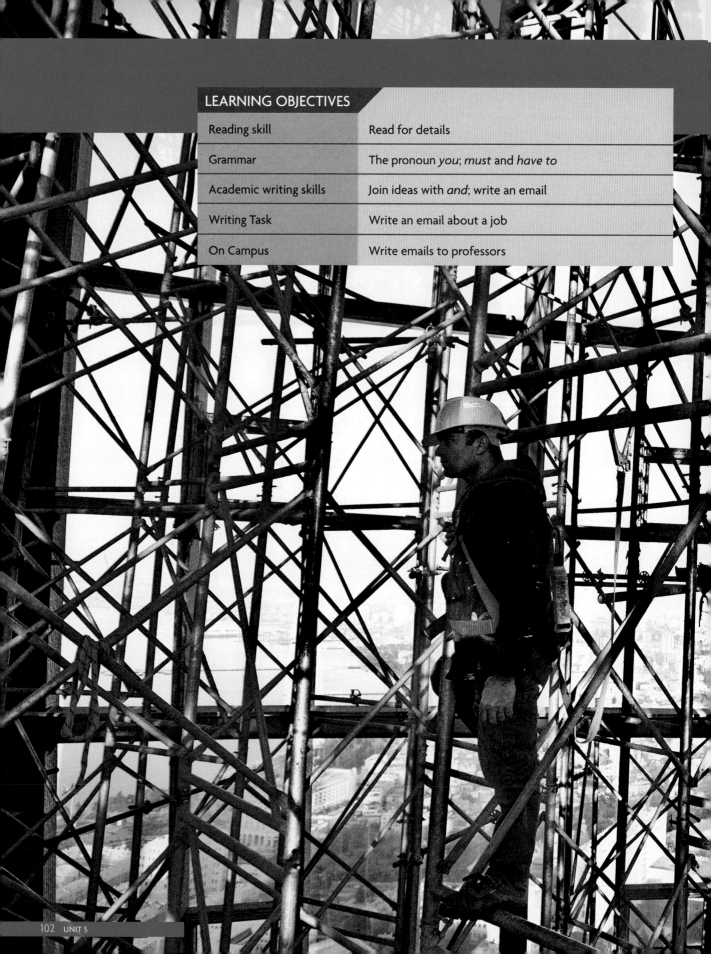

LEARNING OBJECTIVES

Reading skill	Read for details
Grammar	The pronoun *you*; *must* and *have to*
Academic writing skills	Join ideas with *and*; write an email
Writing Task	Write an email about a job
On Campus	Write emails to professors

UNIT 5

ACTIVATE YOUR KNOWLEDGE

Ask and answer the questions with a partner.

1 What do you think the men's jobs are?

2 Do you want this job? Why or why not?

3 What makes a job good?

4 What job do you want? What job do you not want?

PREPARING TO WATCH

1 Work with a partner and answer the questions.

   1 Do you work? What do you do?

   2 What are some unusual jobs?

   3 What are some dangerous jobs?

   4 Would you like to have an unusual job? Why or why not?

2 Look at the pictures from the video. Match the sentence halves.

1 There is a large	**a** much bigger than the man.
2 The truck is carrying	**b** are flying in the air.
3 The truck is	**c** hole in the ground.
4 The dirt and rocks	**d** a lot of rocks and dirt.

GLOSSARY

copper (n) a soft, red-brown metal used to make wires, pipes, etc.

mine (n) a hole in the ground where people dig out gold, coal, etc.

produce (v) to make or grow something

wire (n) a long, very thin piece of metal

dig (v) to make a hole in the ground by moving the dirt away

giant (adj) very big

WHILE WATCHING

3 ▶ Watch the video. Write *T* (true) or *F* (false) next to the statements. Correct the false statements.

_____ 1 The Bingham mine is in Utah.

_____ 2 The mine produces enough copper wires for all the homes in Canada.

_____ 3 We use copper wires in a lot of different places.

_____ 4 The trucks work 12 hours a day.

4 ▶ Watch again. Circle the words you hear.

1 It is the *largest* / *longest* mine of its kind in the world.

2 It is almost *one mile* / *two-and-a-half miles* deep.

3 The rocks contain a *large* / *small* amount of copper.

4 They also use something *stronger* / *weaker* to get the rocks and copper out of the ground.

5 Check (✔) the sentences about work in the Bingham mine. Give reasons for your answers.

1 ☐ It is difficult.

2 ☐ It can be dangerous.

3 ☐ The truck drivers work in the office for half of the day.

4 ☐ The operations manager has an important job.

5 ☐ Finding copper can take a long time.

6 ☐ There are many mines in Utah.

DISCUSSION

6 Work with a partner and answer the questions.

1 Is working in the Bingham mine an interesting job? Why or why not?

2 Are there any mines in your country or region? What do they produce?

3 What other jobs are similar to working in a mine?

UNDERSTANDING
MAIN IDEAS

UNDERSTANDING
DETAILS

MAKING INFERENCES

READING

PREPARING TO READ

USING YOUR KNOWLEDGE

1 Ask and answer the questions with a partner.

1 Where do you find information about jobs?
2 What information do you want to know before you take a job?
3 What makes someone good at his or her job?

2 Look at the texts. Where are they from?

a a website for tourists
b a website for jobs
c a website for food and drinks

UNDERSTANDING KEY VOCABULARY

3 You are going to read online job posts. Read the sentences. Choose the best definition for the words in bold.

1 I am **in shape**. I run every day and ride my bike to work.
  a in good health; strong
  b have a lot of money
2 My mom is a doctor. She works at a **hospital**.
  a a place where people who are sick or hurt go for help
  b a place where people go to study and learn
3 Miriam needs two teaspoons of **medicine**. She is not feeling well.
  a a sandwich or a salad
  b something you take to feel better
4 Oscar is a **pilot**. He learned to fly planes and did well on a flying test.
  a a person who teaches children
  b a person who flies an airplane
5 Basketball players get good **pay**. They make millions of dollars a year.
  a the money you receive for doing a job
  b the feeling you get from doing good work
6 I have **friendly** teachers. They always say "hi" and smile when I see them.
  a nice and kind
  b not nice or kind
7 The **nurse** checked the boy's temperature. He was not feeling well.
  a a person who helps doctors and takes care of people
  b a person who helps children learn at school
8 I am **healthy**. I eat food that is good for me. I get sleep. I take care of myself.
  a quick to understand; smart
  b being well; not sick

Find_my_job.com

FIND A JOB   GET HELP!   UPLOAD YOUR RÉSUMÉ

A

YOUR SEARCH ✕

AREA(S): <u>Medicine</u>

JOB(S): <u>Nurse</u>

✉ <u>Email me jobs like this</u>

🔊 <u>RSS Feeds</u>

LOCATION[1]: Vancouver, British Columbia, Canada

Vancouver Hospital

Vancouver Hospital is part of the British Columbia University School of **Medicine**. We teach doctors and **nurses**.

We are looking for a nurse to work at the hospital and teach student nurses. You have to work early mornings and late nights.

You must have ten years of experience[2]. You must also speak Chinese and English.

Pay: $4,800 per month

Schedule: Monday–Friday and some weekends

B

YOUR SEARCH ✕

AREA(S): <u>Aviation</u>

JOB(S): <u>Pilot</u>

✉ <u>Email me jobs like this</u>

🔊 <u>RSS Feeds</u>

LOCATION: Denver, Colorado, United States

FlyHigh Air Transport Company

FlyHigh is a small company in Denver, Colorado. We have private[3] flights throughout the United States.

We are looking for a **pilot**. All our pilots are **friendly** and speak English and Spanish.

You must have two years of experience. You have to work weekends. You must be **healthy** and **in shape**.

Pay: $130–180 per hour

Schedule: 10–15 hours per week

C

YOUR SEARCH ✕

AREA(S): <u>Education</u>

JOB(S): <u>Teacher</u>

✉ <u>Email me jobs like this</u>

🔊 <u>RSS Feeds</u>

LOCATION: Shelburne, Nova Scotia, Canada

Shelburne Elementary School

Shelburne is a private school in Nova Scotia. Our teachers are friendly and interested in helping children.

We are looking for a math teacher to teach grades 1–3.

You must have a university education. You must speak English.

Pay: $48,000 per year

Schedule: September–June

---

[1]**location** (n) a place
[2]**experience** (n) what you know from doing your job
[3]**private** (adj) belongs to one person or group

WHILE READING

4 Scan the texts. Write words from the texts in the blanks.

	text A	text B	text C
1 What is the job?	(1)	pilot	(2)
2 Which country is the job in?	(3)	(4)	Canada
3 Where is the work?	Vancouver Hospital	(5)	Shelburne Elementary School
4 What is the pay?	$4,800 per month	(6)	(7)
5 What is the schedule?	Monday–Friday and some weekends	10–15 hours per week	(8)

READING FOR DETAILS

SKILLS

Reading for details

Reading for details means looking for key words and information that supports the main idea. Details give more information about the main idea. One way of reading for details is to follow the steps below:

• Ask a question. (e.g., *Vancouver Hospital teaches nurses – is this true or false?*)
• Scan the text to find key words and sentences. (e.g., *Vancouver, teach, nurses*)
• Read the sentences in the paragraph with the key words to find the correct answer. (e.g., *We teach doctors and nurses.*)

PRISM Online Workbook

5 Read the texts again. Write *T* (true) or *F* (false) next to the statements.

_____ 1 The pilot at FlyHigh must speak two languages.
_____ 2 The teacher at Shelburne Elementary School has to teach grade 12.
_____ 3 The nurse at Vancouver Hospital must have ten years of experience.
_____ 4 Teachers at Shelburne Elementary School are friendly.
_____ 5 Pilots at FlyHigh are paid per hour.
_____ 6 The nurse at Vancouver Hospital must speak two languages.

DISCUSSION

6 Work with a partner. Ask and answer the questions.

1 Which jobs need someone who is friendly?
2 Which jobs ask that the person speak more than one language? Why do you think they ask for that?
3 Which job from Reading 1 do you want? Why?

READING 2

PREPARING TO READ

USING YOUR KNOWLEDGE

1 Think about the emails you write to your friends.

    1 Why do you write them?

    2 What do you write about?

    3 Is your language the same when you write as when you speak?

2 Work with a partner. Compare your answers in Exercise 1. What is the same? What is different?

UNDERSTANDING KEY VOCABULARY

3 You are going to read emails about job searches. Read the sentences. Write the words and phrases in bold next to the definitions.

PRISM Online Workbook

    1 Science is very **interesting**. There is so much to learn and know.

    2 I work for a **company** that makes computers.

    3 I'm a math **teacher**. I teach calculus to students at Halifax School.

    4 My university has a music **center**. People take music classes and see music shows there.

    5 My sister is very **good at** basketball. She is the best player on the team.

    6 I need to do well in **high school** so I can go to a good university.

    7 My mom is an **engineer**. She designs and builds parts for cars.

    8 School is **great**. I really like it, and I'm learning a lot. It's going well.

a _____ (n) a person who designs and builds things

b _____ (n) an organization that sells something to make money

c _____ (n) a school for children about 15 to 18 years old

d _____ (adj) able to do something well

e _____ (n) a place with a special purpose

f _____ (adj) very good; excellent

g _____ (n) a person who helps others to learn

h _____ (adj) getting your attention because it is exciting; not boring

A

To: m_evgin@cup.org
From: k_t_b1001@cup.org
Subject: **Interesting** job for you!

Hi, Meng!

I've found a **great** job for you. It's for a dance **teacher**. The job is at David Mitchell's Dance **Center** in Allentown.

You have to get up early in the morning. There are 12 students in each group. You have to be very friendly and **good at** dancing. The pay is very good – they pay $28 an hour. You don't have to work on Saturday or Sunday.

I think you'll like this job. Here's the link[1]: www.dancecompany.org/dance-teacher

Talk to you soon!

Karel

B

To: erik1221@cup.org
From: ingrid_soljberg@cup.org
Subject: IT'S MOM—LOOK AT THIS JOB!

Erik,

I've found a great job for you. It's in Oslo, and I know you want to live there. Here's the link: www.itcompany.org/jobs

I know this **company**.

The job is for a software[2] **engineer**. They pay $65,150 a year!

You must have studied computer science in college, and you have to have 2 years of experience. It also says that you must know some Norwegian. You don't have to speak Norwegian a lot, so it's OK for you.

Let me know what you think!

Love,

Mom

C

To: daria_122@cup.org
From: olly_murgatroyd@cup.org
Subject: Do you want a job in a great country?

Dear Daria,

I hope you're well. I have a great job for you. I think you'll like it. It's in South Korea! I know you love Korean food.

The job is in Yeonggwang. It's a small town in the south of the country.

The job is at a **high school**. You have to teach English and French to grades 10 to 12. You speak English and French (and Russian!).

You don't have to speak Korean, so this is a great job for you. You have to work many hours every day. But you are a very serious teacher. I know you work hard.

Here's the link: www.skoreajobs.com/Education/HS/Languages

Good luck!

Oliver

[1]**link** (n) a word or phrase on a website that takes you to another website
[2]**software** (n) the instructions that control what a computer can do; computer program

WHILE READING

4 Scan the texts. Write the correct information in the blanks.

SCANNING TO FIND INFORMATION

1 The email to Meng is about a job as a _____ .
2 There are _____ students in a dance class at the center.
3 The email to Erik is about a job as a _____ .
4 The pay for Erik's job is $ _____ a year.
5 The job for Daria is in _____ .
6 Daria must teach grades _____ to
_____ .

5 Read the text again. Choose the answer that best states the main ideas.

READING FOR MAIN IDEAS

a Each email is from a company. The company gives information about a job.
b Each email is about a teaching job. The emails talk about the languages the person needs to speak.
c Each email is from a family member or friend. The person talks about a job.
d Each email is from a person looking for a job. The person says why the job is good.

6 Read the texts again. Write *M* (Meng), *E* (Erik), or *D* (Daria) next to the statements.

READING FOR DETAILS

1 He / She must be good at dancing. _____
2 He / She has to teach two languages. _____
3 He / She must have two years of experience. _____
4 He / She has to get up early. _____
5 He / She must work many hours every day. _____

DISCUSSION

7 Work with a partner. Ask and answer the questions.

SYNTHESIZING

1 Which jobs from Reading 2 would you be good at? Why?
2 Which jobs in Reading 2 do you think you need to be healthy and in shape for? Why?
3 What else does each job need a person to be good at?
4 Use ideas from Readings 1 and 2 to answer the question:
  What information is important to know about a job?

PRISM Online Workbook

VOCABULARY FOR JOBS

1 Make sentences about jobs. Write the verb phrases from the box in the correct places in column B of the chart.

> grows food and raises animals   writes news stories
> plays on a sports team   teaches children
> ~~gives people medicine~~
> teaches people to dance   takes care of sick people
> creates software for computers   teaches languages
> manages people

A jobs	B activities	C locations
1 A farmer		on a farm.
2 A manager		
3 A doctor	gives people medicine	
4 A journalist		in towns, cities, and different countries.
5 A software engineer		
6 A basketball player		in big cities.
7 A school teacher		
8 A dance teacher		
9 A nurse		
10 A language teacher		

2 Write the prepositional phrases from the box in the correct places in column C of the chart. The phrases may be used more than once.

> in a hospital.   in an office.   in a school.
> in a center.   in a company.

ADJECTIVE PHRASES

LANGUAGE

An *adjective phrase* describes the subject of the sentence. The adjective phrase comes after a form of the verb *be*. One type of adjective phrase is *very* + adjective.

Software engineers have to be **very smart**. Nurses must be **very kind**. Another type of adjective phrase is adjective + *and* + adjective.

Pilots must be **healthy and in shape**. Nurses have to be **kind and helpful**.

Adjectives with prepositional phrases

Another type of adjective phrase is *good at* + noun or *good with* + noun.

The teacher has to be **good at math**. Nurses must be **good with people**.

Usually people are *good at* a subject and *good with* a person or object.

PRISM Online Workbook

3 Read the sentences and circle the best words and phrases.

1 Dance teachers have to be *interesting / healthy and strong*. They are moving around all day!
2 Doctors must be *very smart / very healthy and strong*. There is a lot to know about medicine.
3 Nurses have to be *friendly / strong*. They work with people.
4 Farmers have to be *strong / friendly*. They work with animals and equipment.

4 Circle the correct preposition in each sentence.

1 An elementary school teacher has to be good *at / with* children.
2 A software engineer needs to be good *at / with* computers.
3 A nurse needs to be good *at / with* people.
4 A French and Spanish teacher needs to be good *at / with* languages.
5 A journalist needs to be good *at / with* writing.

WRITING

CRITICAL THINKING

At the end of this unit, you are going to do the Writing Task below.

> Write an email about a job.

Using a Likert scale

A *scale* is a way to measure something. In a Likert scale, you read a statement and then circle the answer that is true for you. Your answer shows how you feel.

I am good at English.

1   2   3   ④   5

1 = strongly disagree
2 = disagree
3 = neither agree nor disagree

4 = agree
5 = strongly agree

 EVALUATE

1 Read the statements and circle the answers that are true for you.

1 = strongly disagree
2 = disagree
3 = neither agree nor disagree

4 = agree
5 = strongly agree

1 I am healthy and in shape.
1   2   3   4   5

2 I am good at dancing.
1   2   3   4   5

3 I am good with people.
1   2   3   4   5

4 I am very smart.
1   2   3   4   5

5 I am kind and helpful.
1   2   3   4   5

6 I am good with children.
1   2   3   4   5

7 I am very good at basketball.
1   2   3   4   5

8 I am good at math.
1   2   3   4   5

9 I am good at writing.
1   2   3   4   5

10 I am good with computers.
1   2   3   4   5

11 I am good with animals.
1   2   3   4   5

12 I am good at languages.
1   2   3   4   5

2 Work with a partner. Underline the adjective phrases in the statements in Exercise 1.

3 Look at the jobs. For each job, write the adjective phrase(s) from Exercise 1 that describe(s) it. The first one has been done for you.

ANALYZE ▲

A jobs	B best description
1 a farmer	healthy and in shape
2 a manager	
3 a doctor	
4 a journalist	
5 a software engineer	
6 a basketball player	
7 a school teacher	
8 a dance teacher	
9 a nurse	
10 a language teacher	

4 Work with a partner. Read your partner's answers to the questionnaire. Then look at the chart in Exercise 3 and choose the best job for your partner.

EVALUATE ▲

THE PRONOUN *YOU*

LANGUAGE

Use the pronoun *you* to say something to someone. Use *you* in emails and in job postings.

You have to work many hours. **You** are a very serious teacher. **You** work hard.

You can be singular or plural.

Singular	Plural
You have to work weekends. (*you* = 1 person)	*You* have to work weekends. (*you* = more than 1 person)

The verb does not change. It is the same form.

PRISM **Online** Workbook

1 Rewrite the information in the sentences. Use *you* as the subject of each sentence.

1 He must have three years of experience.

_____

2 She is kind and good with people.

_____

3 We have a university education.

_____

4 They speak Chinese.

_____

MUST AND *HAVE TO*

LANGUAGE

Use *must* + base verb form or *have to* + base verb form to say that something is necessary.

Doctors **must be** smart. Doctors **have to be** smart.

Use *must* + base verb form for *I, you, he, she, it, we,* and *they.* Never use *must to* + base verb form.

A nurse **must be** kind and helpful.

Use *have to* + base verb form for *I, you, we,* and *they.*

Managers **have to be** good with people. They **have to be** good with people.

Use *has to* + base verb form for *he, she,* and *it.*

A manager **has to be** good with people. He **has to be** good with people.

2 Correct the mistakes in the sentences.

1 A basketball player musts be strong and healthy.

_____

2 Pilots have work at night.

_____

3 A manager have to be helpful.

_____

4 Teachers must good with people.

_____

5 A software engineer must to be good at math.

_____

6 Farmers have good with animals.

_____

7 Journalists must to good at writing.

_____

8 A language teacher must good at speaking and writing.

_____

Do not have to and must not

Use *do not have to / does not have to* + base verb form to say that something is not necessary.

Use *do not have to* + base verb form for *I, you, we,* and *they.*
Farmers **do not have to be** good with computers.

Use *does not have to* + base verb form for *he, she,* and *it.*
A language teacher **does not have to be** good at math.

Use *must not* + base verb form to say that something is not allowed.
You **must not be** late!

3 Put the words in order to make sentences.

1 does / have to / A farmer / with people / not / be good / .

_____

2 A software engineer / does not / be / patient and / kind / have to / .

_____

3 with animals / have / not / do / Nurses / to be good / .

_____

4 be strong / You / not / have to / do / .

_____

5 A French teacher / have to / good / at math / be / does not / .

_____

6 good / You / do not / have to / be / at calculus / .

_____

ACADEMIC WRITING SKILLS

JOINING IDEAS WITH *AND*

Simple sentences

A *simple sentence* has a subject and a verb.

subject verb   subject verb
You are friendly. You are good with people.

When the subjects and verbs in two sentences are the same, you can join these ideas with *and* in one sentence. You only need the subject once.

and
You are friendly. You are good with people. →
You are friendly **and** good with people.

Writing compound sentences with *and*

When the subjects are different in two simple sentences, you can join these together with *and* in one sentence. This is called a *compound sentence*.

You still need both subjects. Put a comma before *and*.

subject verb   subject verb
The pay is good. The job is fun. →

, and
The pay is good. The job is fun. →
The pay is good, **and** the job is fun.

It is important to have a mix of sentence types in your writing. Using compound sentences can help your writing be better.

PRISM Online Workbook

1 Rewrite the simple sentences. If the subjects are the same, join the ideas with *and* in one sentence. If the subjects are different, write one compound sentence with *and*.

1 You must be smart. You must be good with people.

_____

2 You have to be healthy. You have to be strong.

_____

3 Dance teachers have to be in shape. You are in shape.

_____

4 The job is to teach English. You are an English and French teacher.

_____

WRITING AN EMAIL

Begin an email with a greeting.

Hi, Meng!	Use *Hi* for people you know. Use an exclamation point to show excitement.
Erik,	Use a person's first name, followed by a comma for most situations.
Dear Daria,	Use *Dear* for coworkers or people you know, but not that well.

End an email with a closing. Write your name after the closing.

Talk to you soon! Karel	Use this expression for people you talk to often.
Love, Mom	Use this for close family and friends.
Good luck! Oliver	Use this phrase when wishing a person well.

Use contractions in informal emails to family and friends.

You do not have to work on Saturday or Sunday. → You **don't** have to work on Saturday or Sunday.

I think you will like this job → I think **you'll** like this job.

It is in South Korea. → **It's** in South Korea.

I hope you are doing well. → I hope **you're** doing well.

I have found a great job for you. → **I've** found a great job for you.

2 Rewrite the information below into emails with a greeting, sentences with contractions, and a closing.

1 To: Allen
Sentences: I am excited to see you soon. I think you will like my news!
From: Max

2 To: Jen
Sentences: You do not have to worry. I found a job for you. It is in London!
From: Carmen

3 To: Chuanwei
Sentences: It is great that you found a job! I think you will be so happy there.
From: Tao

WRITING TASK

PRISM Online Workbook   ▸ Write an email about a job.

PLAN

1 Look at the job you chose for your partner in the Critical Thinking section. Think of details for the job and fill in the chart.

Who is the job for?	
What is the job?	
Where is the job?	
What does he / she need to be good at?	
Why is your friend good for the job?	
What is the pay?	
When does he / she work?	

2 Refer to the Task Checklist as you prepare your email.

WRITE A FIRST DRAFT

3 Now use the information from your chart to write an email to your partner about the job. Use language for emails to help you.

To:
From:
Subject:

_____ (greeting)
I hope you're well. I have a great job for you. _____

_____

_____

_____

_____

_____

_____

_____

_____

_____

_____

_____

(sentences about the job with information from Exercise 1)
Here's the link: www.discoverjobs4you.com
_____ ! (closing)

_____

EDIT

4 Use the Task Checklist to edit your email.

TASK CHECKLIST	✔
Describe the job and explain why it is good for your partner.	
Use adjective phrases to describe the person for the job.	
Use *must* and *have to* to say that something is necessary.	
Use the pronoun *you* and contractions in your email.	
Use a greeting and closing in your email.	

5 Make any necessary changes to your email.

ON CAMPUS

WRITING EMAILS TO PROFESSORS

Writing emails

Students often write emails to their professors to ask for help or permission. They need to be polite. They should also give complete information and good reasons.

PREPARING TO READ

1 Work with a partner and answer the questions.

1 Do you write email messages to your professors? What do you write about?

2 Look at the reasons below. When is it okay to write to a professor?

☐ You are sick and you want to know the homework assignment.

☐ You don't like your project group.

☐ You want to turn in your homework late.

☐ You need help with a lesson.

☐ You aren't ready for a test. You don't want to take it on the test day.

3 Are you nervous when you write to a professor or teacher? Why / Why not?

WHILE READING

2 Read the two email messages.

Subject: Appointment request

Dear Professor Thompson,

I am a student in your Math 124 class. I don't understand today's lesson. I need some help, so I want to talk to you, please. Your office hours[1] are from 2:30 – 4:30, but I have to work at the library then. Could I make an appointment[2] at 1:30?

Sincerely,
Magda Koch

Subject: Hi from Lily

Hi,

I'm Lily. I have a lot of homework. Also, I have to take a test in another class tomorrow. I wanna turn in my project next week. Okay?

Lily

---

[1] **office hours** (n) the time a professor is in their office ready to talk to students

[2] **make an appointment** (phr) agree on a time to see someone

3 Work with a partner. Answer the questions.

1 What does Magda want to do?
2 When does Magda want to meet? Why?
3 What does Lily want to do?
4 What is Lily's reason?

4 Check (✔) the correct name.

Which student ...	Magda	Lily
a is polite?	_____	_____
b writes the class name?	_____	_____
c uses slang?	_____	_____
d writes her full name?	_____	_____
e writes her professor's name?	_____	_____
f gives a good reason?	_____	_____

PRACTICE

5 Complete the email to a teacher. Use your own ideas.

> To:
> From:
> Subject:
>
> Dear _____ ,
> I am in your _____ class. We have a quiz on Friday, but
> I have to _____ at the same time. Could I take the quiz
> on Thursday?
> _____ ,
> Jennifer Mapes

6 Work with a partner. Read your partner's email and answer the questions.

1 What does your partner have to do?
2 Is it a good reason? Why / Why not?
3 Is he / she polite?

REAL-WORLD APPLICATION

7 Work with a partner. Look at the list of reasons in Exercise 1. Choose a reason and write an email to your professor.

8 Read your partner's email. Is it a good email? Is he / she polite?

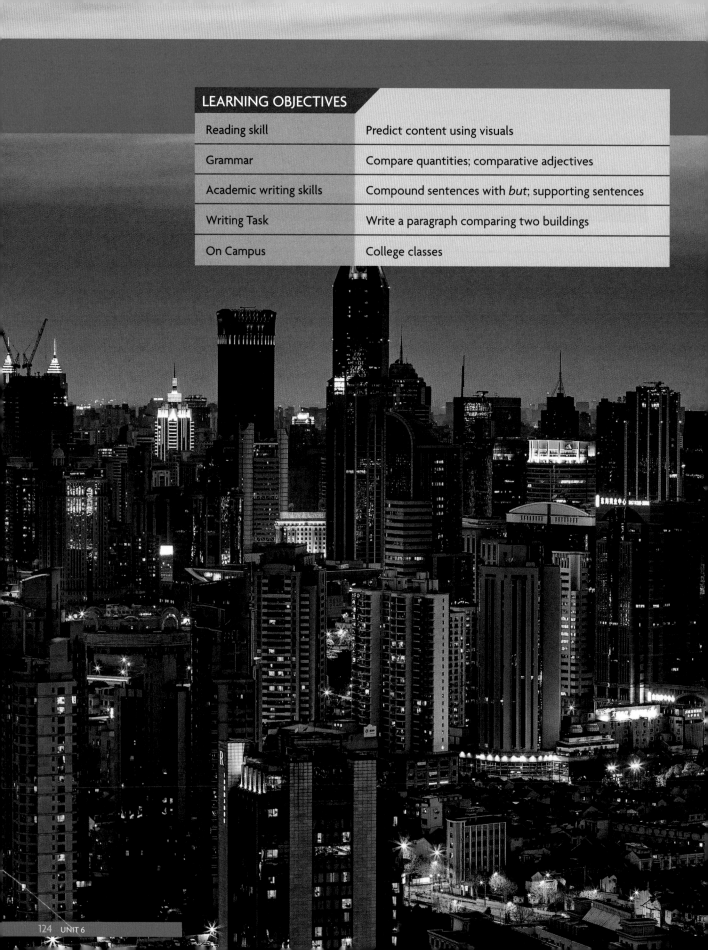

LEARNING OBJECTIVES

Reading skill	Predict content using visuals
Grammar	Compare quantities; comparative adjectives
Academic writing skills	Compound sentences with *but*; supporting sentences
Writing Task	Write a paragraph comparing two buildings
On Campus	College classes

HOMES AND BUILDINGS

ACTIVATE YOUR KNOWLEDGE

Work with a partner. Ask and answer the questions below.

1 Do you think this city looks like a nice place to live? Why or why not?

2 How is this city like or not like your town or city?

3 Do you like being in very big cities? Why or why not?

PREPARING TO WATCH

ACTIVATING YOUR KNOWLEDGE

1 Work with a partner. Write the name of a famous tall building for each country.

Canada	Mexico	Italy	Dubai, UAE	China

PREDICTING CONTENT USING VISUALS

2 Look at the pictures from the video. Match the pictures (1–4) to the countries.

a England _____
b United States _____
c France _____
d Egypt _____

> **GLOSSARY**
>
> **stone** (n) a hard, natural substance that is found in the ground
>
> **cathedral** (n) a large and important church
>
> **spire** (n) a tall, pointed tower on the top of a building such as a church
>
> **steel** (n) a very strong metal made from iron
>
> **skyscraper** (n) a very tall building

WHILE WATCHING

3 ▶ Watch the video. Put the buildings in order (1–5) from the oldest to the newest.

a Lincoln Cathedral _____
b Eiffel Tower _____
c Great Pyramid _____
d Taipei 101 _____
e Chrysler Building _____

UNDERSTANDING MAIN IDEAS

4 ▶ Watch again. Circle the correct answer.

1 The Great Pyramid of Egypt is *445 / 455* feet tall.
2 The Lincoln Cathedral was 46 feet taller than the *Great Pyramid / Eiffel Tower*.
3 The Chrysler Building used *stone / steel* to make it the tallest skyscraper in 1930.
4 The Petronas Towers in Kuala Lumpur, Malaysia are made of glass, steel, and *stone / concrete*.

UNDERSTANDING DETAILS

5 Using the information in the video, check (✔) the true statements.

1 ☐ Buildings are getting taller.
2 ☐ Buildings do not change very much.
3 ☐ New materials help us build taller buildings.
4 ☐ New buildings use more glass than old buildings.
5 ☐ Skyscrapers are common in large cities.
6 ☐ There will be more skyscrapers in the future.

MAKING INFERENCES

DISCUSSION

6 Work with a partner and answer the questions.

1 Have you visited any of the buildings in the video? If so, which one(s)?
2 Which building would you like to visit the most? Why?
3 Describe the tallest building in your city.

READING

READING 1

USING YOUR
KNOWLEDGE

UNDERSTANDING
KEY VOCABULARY

PREPARING TO READ

1 Ask and answer the questions with a partner.

1 What do you like about your home?
2 What kind of home do you want to live in?
3 What makes a home a good place to live?

2 You are going to read an interview with an architect. Read the sentences. Write the words in bold below the photos.

1 In a **garden**, you grow flowers and plants.
2 Children drink out of **plastic** cups.
3 Cities have **tall** buildings.
4 Tables and chairs are made of **wood**.
5 The **roof** on our house is red.
6 I have a picture on the **wall**.
7 The sun shines through the **window**.
8 Be careful. **Glass** can break.

_____ _____ _____ _____

_____ _____ _____ _____

PREDICTING CONTENT USING VISUALS

> *Visuals* can be photographs, pictures, graphs, or charts. You can use the visuals to help you understand the topic of the text.

3 Look at the photos. Circle the phrases to make statements you agree with.

PRISM Online Workbook

I think the buildings in the photos are ...

a exciting.

b easy to build.

c good for people to live in.

d in the same city.

Architect's World
EXPERT INTERVIEW

1 ***Professor Michael Chan*** *teaches design to architects at the London School of Architecture. He has been at the school for 30 years. There have been many changes in home design in the last 30 years. This week, Michael Chan tells us more about new home design around the world.*

The architect, Michael Chan, makes drawings for houses.

Japanese roof house

garden home with plants

mirror house

2 ***Architect's World***: What are your favorite home designs?
Michael Chan: I really like Japanese designs. Many people in Japan build interesting houses. For example, the roof house is very **tall** and has a steep[1] **roof**. The **windows** on the roof are different sizes. Inside the house, the rooms are very narrow[2], and the ceilings[3] are very high. It is simple and very small inside.

3 ***AW***: What do you think about "green"[4] homes?
MC: It is very important to build houses that are good for the Earth. My favorite example is a house in Saigon, Vietnam. It is a "garden home." This house is in the middle of a busy city, but there are plants everywhere. From the street, people see a tall **garden**. But, in fact, it is a house. There are plants and trees in front of the glass **walls**. There is also a small garden on top of the roof. You can put chairs and a table there and enjoy tea with your family.

4 ***AW***: What do architects use to build houses?
MC: Many architects use **wood**. It keeps your house warm in winter. They also use metal[5] and **glass**. Sometimes they use something different. For example, one architect from Amsterdam put mirrors on every wall of a house. Other architects use glass or even **plastic** for the walls.

[1]**steep** (adj) goes down very quickly and almost straight down
[2]**narrow** (adj) not much space from one side to the other
[3]**ceilings** (n) the inside top of a room that you see when you look up
[4]**green** (adj) something that is good for the Earth and does not use a lot of energy
[5]**metal** (adj) a hard and shiny material, such as iron or gold

WHILE READING

SCANNING TO FIND
INFORMATION

4 Read the text. Check (✔) the boxes in the chart that are true for the two houses.

	windows are different sizes	has glass walls	has a small garden on the roof	rooms are narrow
Japanese roof house				
Vietnamese "garden home"				

READING FOR
MAIN IDEAS

5 Match the sentence parts to create a main idea.

1 Michael Chan likes	**a** metal, wood, glass, and plastic.
2 Green architecture is	**b** good for the Earth.
3 Architects make homes out of	**c** unusual and interesting homes.

READING FOR DETAILS

6 Read the interview again. Write *T* (true) or *F* (false) next to the statements.

_____ **1** Professor Chan's favorite home designs are Korean.

_____ **2** The roof house has small and narrow rooms.

_____ **3** Professor Chan says it is important to build more homes in Vietnam.

_____ **4** The "garden home" is in the center of a big city.

_____ **5** Gardens and plants are good for the Earth.

_____ **6** In Amsterdam, many architects put mirrors on the walls.

DISCUSSION

7 Ask and answer the questions with a partner.

1 What do you think makes a home good for the Earth?

2 Which home from the photos would you like to live in? Why?

3 Why do you think the architect from Amsterdam used mirrors?

READING 2

PREPARING TO READ

USING YOUR
KNOWLEDGE

1 Tell a partner if you agree or disagree with each statement. Explain why.

1 It's important for the buildings in a city to look interesting.
2 Tall buildings are better than small buildings.
3 It is fun to be high up in a building.

UNDERSTANDING
KEY VOCABULARY

2 You are going to read an article about skyscrapers. Read the sentences. Write the words in bold next to the correct definitions.

1 The car is too **expensive**. I don't have the money to buy it.
2 The **buildings** in my city are made of metal and glass – both the stores and the offices.
3 You can take an **elevator** to the top of the building. It is very high!
4 I live in an **apartment** on the fourth floor.
5 How much does this TV **cost**? I can't see the price.
6 A plane ticket to Boston is very **cheap**! I bought it for only $54!

PRISM Online Workbook

a _____ (adj) costing a lot of money
b _____ (n) a house, school, office, or store with a roof and walls
c _____ (adj) costing little money
d _____ (n) a set of rooms for someone to live in on one level of a building or house
e _____ (v) to have an amount of money as a price that someone must pay
f _____ (n) a machine, like a small room, that carries people straight up or down in a tall building

Skyscrapers

What Are Skyscrapers?

1 Skyscrapers are very tall **buildings**. They are usually more than 984 feet (300 meters) tall. You can see skyscrapers in cities around the world. Many countries build skyscrapers so tourists go there. There are many skyscrapers in Asia, the Middle East, the Americas, and Europe. Inside a skyscraper, there are offices, stores, restaurants, and **apartments**.

What Are Some Famous Skyscrapers?

2 The Empire State Building in New York is a world-famous skyscraper. It has two million visitors every year. It is popular with tourists, but there are taller and more modern skyscrapers in the Middle East and in Asia. The Shanghai World Financial Center, One World Trade Center in New York City, and the Burj Khalifa in Dubai are taller than the Empire State Building. The Burj Khalifa is taller than the Shanghai World Financial Center and One World Trade Center. One World Trade Center is taller than the Shanghai World Financial Center. One World Trade Center is more modern than the other two buildings. It opened in 2014.

How Much Money Do Skyscrapers Cost?

3 Skyscrapers are very **expensive**. They cost more money than other buildings. The Burj Khalifa cost $1,500,000,000 to build. It was more expensive than the Shanghai World Financial Center ($850,000,000), but it was **cheaper** than One World Trade Center. One World Trade Center cost $3,900,000,000.

What Is Inside a Skyscraper?

4 The Burj Khalifa has 163 floors. This is more than One World Trade Center or the Shanghai World Financial Center. One World Trade Center has 104 floors and the Shanghai World Financial Center has 101 floors. All skyscrapers have **elevators**. The Burj Khalifa has more elevators than One World Trade Center or the Shanghai World Financial Center. It has 57 elevators. One World Trade Center has 54 elevators, but the Shanghai World Financial Center has fewer. It only has 31. Many skyscrapers also have shopping malls inside them. A lot of people come to shop every day.

Shanghai World Financial Center, 2008 (1614 feet)

One World Trade Center, 2014 (1776 feet)

Burj Khalifa, 2010 (2717 feet)

WHILE READING

SCANNING TO FIND INFORMATION

3 Scan the text. Write words from the text in the chart.

	Shanghai World Financial Center	One World Trade Center	Burj Khalifa
A city	Shanghai	New York	(1)_____
B height (ft)	(2)_____	(3)_____	2,717
C year	2008	2014	2010
D number of floors	(4)_____	104	163
E number of elevators	(5)_____	54	57
F cost (USD)	$850,000,000	(6)$_____	$1,500,000,000

READING FOR DETAILS

4 Follow the directions to annotate the text.

1 Underline the four questions in italics the text asks.
2 Underline key words in each paragraph that answer the question.
3 Compare your answers with a partner.

DISCUSSION

SYNTHESIZING

5 Ask and answer the questions with a partner. Look at the photos and the text.

1 Which skyscraper was the most expensive to build? Why do you think it was so expensive?
2 Why do you think skyscrapers need so many elevators?
3 Use information from Reading 1 and Reading 2 to answer the question: What information do architects need to make a building or a home?

⊙ LANGUAGE DEVELOPMENT

PRONOUNS

You can match pronouns to nouns to help you understand a text.

Skyscrapers are very tall buildings. **They** [They = Skyscrapers] are usually more than 984 ft (300 m) tall.
The Empire State Building in New York is a world-famous skyscraper.
It [It = The Empire State Building] has two million visitors every year.

1 Read the text on page 132 again. Match the words and phrases in the box to the pronouns in bold in the sentences.

> Burj Khalifa   One World Trade Center
> Shanghai World Financial Center   skyscrapers

1 **It** was more expensive than the Shanghai World Financial Center ($850,000,000). _____
2 **It** opened in 2014. _____
3 **They** cost more money than other buildings. _____
4 **It** has only 31 elevators. _____

VOCABULARY FOR BUILDINGS

2 Read the sentences and write the words from the box in the blanks.

> apartments   ceiling   elevators   entrance   exit
> garden   parking lot   roof   shopping mall
> stairs   walls   windows

1 There are over 520 different stores in the Mall of America, which is a _____ in Minnesota.
2 In the Burj Khalifa, there are over 900 _____ you can live in.
3 It is popular for a building to have a _____ on the _____ . The plants on top of the building are good for the city.
4 The John Hancock Center in Chicago has a race up the building. People run up the _____ .
5 Skyscrapers often have one main _____ at the front of the building. It is also the _____ . You leave from there, too.
6 One World Trade Center has 13,000 glass _____ .
7 Each floor in the One World Trade Center is nine feet high from floor to _____ .
8 There are 1,100 parking spaces in the _____ at Shanghai World Financial Center.
9 The _____ of skyscrapers have to be very strong. They hold the building up.
10 Skyscrapers must have _____ . They are too tall for people to walk up the stairs.

3 Read the sentences and circle the correct words.

1 You can leave your car in the *garden / parking lot*.
2 You can ride on the *elevator / stairs* to the next floor.
3 You go into a building through the *entrance / exit*.
4 You can walk up the *elevator / stairs* to the next floor.
5 You must go to the *entrance / exit* to get out if there is a fire.
6 I live in an *apartment / shopping* in the city.
7 I have beautiful pictures on my *ceiling / walls*.
8 The *windows / roof* in my house are made of glass.

ADJECTIVES

4 Match the adjectives to their opposites.

PRISM Online Workbook

1 big	**a** ugly
2 tall	**b** cheap
3 traditional	**c** short
4 old	**d** small
5 expensive	**e** modern
6 beautiful	**f** new

5 Write the adjectives from the box in the correct blanks.

beautiful   cheap   expensive   modern   traditional   ugly

1 It is _____ to build skyscrapers. They are not cheap.
2 Buildings with glass look _____ . They shine in the sun.
3 Skyscrapers are _____ buildings. They are new and interesting.
4 Some homes in China are _____ . They look like homes from the past.
5 It is hard to find a _____ apartment in the city. They cost too much money.
6 Most people like skyscrapers, but I think they are _____ . I prefer small buildings and more traditional designs.

WRITING

CRITICAL THINKING

At the end of this unit, you are going to do the Writing Task below.

▶ Write a comparison of two buildings.

SKILLS

Comparison of data

Data is facts or information. Data is often numbers. If we compare the facts or information about two or more things, we make a comparison of data.

 UNDERSTAND

1 Read the sentences and match them to the row with the same data in the chart on page 133. Write the letter of the row at the end of the sentence it matches.

1 The Burj Khalifa cost $1,500,000,000 to build. It was more expensive than the Shanghai World Financial Center ($850,000,000), but it was cheaper than One World Trade Center. One World Trade Center cost $3,900,000,000. _____

2 The Burj Khalifa has 163 floors. This is more than One World Trade Center or the Shanghai World Financial Center. One World Trade Center has 104 floors, and the Shanghai World Financial Center has 101 floors. _____

3 The Burj Khalifa has more elevators than One World Trade Center or the Shanghai World Financial Center. It has 57 elevators. One World Trade Center has 54 elevators, but the Shanghai World Financial Center has fewer. It only has 31. _____

2 Work with a partner. Choose two skyscrapers you are interested in. Find information on the Internet to complete the chart.

CREATE ▲

	_____ (building 1)	_____ (building 2)
city		
height (ft)		
year		
number of floors		
number of elevators		
cost (USD)		

3 Work with a partner. Ask and answer the questions about your buildings.

ANALYZE ▲

1 Which building is taller?

_____

_____

2 Which building is more modern?

_____

_____

3 Which building is has more floors?

_____

_____

4 Which building has more elevators?

_____

_____

5 Which building was more expensive?

_____

_____

GRAMMAR FOR WRITING

COMPARING QUANTITIES

LANGUAGE

You can compare quantities with *more / fewer / less* + a noun or a noun phrase + *than*. This phrase comes after the subject and the verb.

Use *more* for a higher quantity.

One World Trace Center has **more elevators than** the Shanghai World Financial Center.
Skyscrapers cost **more money than** other buildings.
The garden home in Saigon has **more rooms than** the roof house.

Use *fewer* or *less* for a lower quantity. Use *fewer* with count nouns, and use *less* with noncount nouns.

The Shanghai World Financial Center has **fewer elevators than** One World Trade Center.
There is **less information** about Building B **than** about Building A.

PRISM Online Workbook

1 Put the words and phrases in order to make sentences.

1 The Burj Khalifa / more / floors / than One World Trade Center / has / .

_____

_____

2 visitors / than / has / The Burj Khalifa / the Shanghai World Financial Center / more / .

_____

_____

3 more / than the Mall of America / The John Hancock Center / has / stairs / .

_____

_____

4 has / than the Shanghai World Financial Center / elevators / more / The Burj Khalifa / .

_____

_____

5 money / cost / One World Trade Center / than the Burj Khalifa / more / .

_____

_____

6 Burj Khalifa / less / money / cost / than One World Trade Center / .

_____

_____

COMPARATIVE ADJECTIVES

Use comparative adjectives to describe how two things are different.

For one syllable adjectives, add -(e)r + than.

tall → taller than

The Burj Khalifa is **taller than** the Shanghai World Financial Center.

The roof house is **smaller than** the garden home.

For adjectives with two syllables that end in a consonant + -y, replace the -y with -i and add -er + than.

busy → busier than

Shanghai is **busier than** Kansas City.

For adjectives with two or more syllables, use more + adjective + than or less + adjective + than.

expensive → more expensive than
         → less expensive than

One World Trade Center was **more expensive than** the Burj Khalifa.

The Burj Khalifa was **less expensive than** One World Trade Center.

2 Correct the mistakes in the sentences.

PRISM Online Workbook

1 The Metropolitan Museum of Art in New York is popular the Art Institute of Chicago.

_____

2 One World Trade Center is more of modern the Empire State Building.

_____

3 The John Hancock Center in Chicago is more small the Shanghai World Financial Center.

_____

4 Modern buildings are beautifuler that traditional buildings.

_____

5 The Burj Khalifa taller the One World Trade Center.

_____

6 Wood is more expensive that plastic.

_____

7 This street is many busy than the main road.

_____

8 Many buildings in New York are more old than buildings in Kansas City.

_____

ACADEMIC WRITING SKILLS

COMPOUND SENTENCES WITH *BUT*

A sentence always has a subject and a verb. You can use *but* to join two simple sentences to make a compound sentence. *But* makes a comparison.

Sentences 1 and 2:

subject   *verb*   *subject*   *verb*

One World Trade Center is tall. The Burj Khalifa is taller than One World Trade Center.

Join sentences 1 and 2 with *but*. Add a comma before *but*:

One World Trade Center is tall, **but** the Burj Khalifa is taller than One World Trade Center.

Do not repeat *than* + noun phrase after a comparison:

One World Trade Center is tall, **but** the Burj Khalifa is taller ~~than One World Trade Center~~.

New sentence:

One World Trade Center is tall, **but** the Burj Khalifa is taller.

PRISM Online Workbook

1 Join each pair of simple sentences below to make one compound sentence with *but*.

1 The Shanghai World Financial Center has over 101 floors. One World Trade Center has more floors.

_____

_____

2 The Sears Tower is tall. The CN Tower in Toronto is taller than the Sears Tower.

_____

_____

3 One World Trade Center has many elevators. The Burj Khalifa has more elevators than One World Trade Center.

_____

_____

4 The Art Institute of Chicago has many pictures. The Metropolitan Museum of Art has more pictures than the Art Institute of Chicago.

_____

_____

SUPPORTING SENTENCES

Supporting sentences are in the middle of the paragraph and explain the topic sentence to the reader. Supporting sentences give details and examples to make the topic sentence clearer. All supporting sentences should be related to the topic sentence.

topic sentence	Skyscrapers are very expensive.
supporting sentences and details	They cost more money than other buildings. The Burj Khalifa cost $1,500,000,000 to build. It was more expensive than the Shanghai World Financial Center ($850,000,000), but it was cheaper than One World Trade Center. One World Trade Center cost $3,900,000,000.

2 Read the topic sentence. Check (✔) the supporting sentences and details that explain the topic sentence.

PRISM Online Workbook

1 **topic sentence:** Skyscrapers are very tall buildings.

_____ They are usually more than 984 feet (300 meters) tall.

_____ The Burj Khalifa has more elevators than One World Trade Center or the Shanghai World Financial Center.

_____ Many countries build skyscrapers so tourists go there.

_____ There are many skyscrapers in Asia, the Middle East, the Americas, and Europe.

2 **topic sentence:** All skyscrapers have elevators.

_____ The Burj Khalifa has more elevators than One World Trade Center or the Shanghai World Financial Center.

_____ It has 57 elevators.

_____ One World Trade Center cost $3,900,000,000.

_____ The Empire State Building in New York is a world-famous skyscraper.

_____ One World Trade Center has 54 elevators, but the Shanghai World Financial Center has fewer.

3 Read the topic sentence. Find a supporting sentence in Reading 1 or Reading 2 for the topic sentence.

   1 **topic sentence:** Skyscrapers are very tall.
   supporting sentence:

_____

   2 **topic sentence:** It is important to build houses that are good for the Earth.
   supporting sentence:

_____

4 Read the topic sentence. Write a supporting sentence to explain the topic sentence.

   1 **topic sentence:** Modern design is interesting.
   supporting sentence:

_____

   2 **topic sentence:** Skyscrapers are very expensive.
   supporting sentence:

_____

WRITING TASK

PRISM Online Workbook

Write a comparison of two buildings.

PLAN

1 Look at the chart you completed in the Critical Thinking section. What other information do you want to compare? Add it below.

	(building 1)	(building 2)
_____		
_____		

2 Refer to the Task Checklist as you prepare your paragraph.

WRITE A FIRST DRAFT

3 Write sentences for each topic. Use the information in your chart from the Critical Thinking section and from Exercise 1.

1 Write the names of your buildings. Write what city they are in.
2 Compare the height of your buildings.
3 Compare the year your buildings opened.
4 Compare the number of floors in your buildings.
5 Compare the number of elevators in your buildings.
6 Compare the cost of your buildings.
7 Compare any other information you have.

EDIT

4 Use the Task Checklist to edit your paragraph.

TASK CHECKLIST	✔
Use supporting sentences and details to explain the topic sentence and compare two different buildings.	
Use pronouns to refer to your buildings.	
Use sentences which compare quantities.	
Make sure sentences have *than* after a comparative adjective.	
Join sentences with *but* to make comparisons.	

5 Make any necessary changes to your paragraph.

ON CAMPUS

COLLEGE CLASSES

SKILLS

Class information

In colleges, there are different kinds of classrooms. There are big lecture halls and small science labs. There are also different kinds of teachers. Some are professors, and some are graduate students. The graduate students are usually called TAs (teaching assistants).

PREPARING TO READ

1 Work with a partner. Discuss the questions below.

1 In your country, are classes different sizes?
2 Do you speak or listen more?
3 What are your favorite classes?
4 Do you think college students in your country read more or less for their classes than in North America?

WHILE READING

2 Read the class descriptions and the notes from the academic advisor[1].

BIOLOGY 148 **Human Biology**

Maximum: 650 students

- main class in big lecture hall[2], Tuesday and Thursday, all students together with professor
- small lab class, once a week, 15 students each, with TA
- one book, 480 pages

SOCIOLOGY 150 **Social Problems**

Maximum: 85 students

- main class in small lecture hall, Monday & Wednesday, all students together with professor
- quiz section in classroom, once a week, 12 students each, with TA
- must buy course pack with 27 journal articles
- a lot of writing

ENGLISH 132 **Intro to American Literature**

Maximum: 12 students

- seminar class, every day with professor
- a lot of discussion
- must read 8 novels

[1]**academic advisor** (n) a person who helps students with education plans

[2]**lecture hall** (n) a large classroom in a college

3 Write *T* (true) or *F* (false) next to the statements below.

_____ 1 A lecture is bigger than a quiz section.

_____ 2 A TA teaches a lecture class.

_____ 3 In the English class, students talk a lot.

_____ 4 A course pack is a kind of book.

_____ 5 A professor teaches a lab class.

_____ 6 There is a lot of reading in all the classes.

PRACTICE

4 Complete the email message with the words in the box.

| quiz section   seminar   lab class   lecture |

Subject: My semester schedule

Hi Samim,

How is your class schedule this semester? I'm really busy! I have an economics class. There is a big (1)_____ with the professor on Tuesday and Thursday mornings. I think there are 400 students! On Monday and Wednesday, we have a (2)_____ with a TA. That class is small, so I get a lot of help.

My chemistry class is really hard. The professor talks so fast! But I like the (3)_____ because the TA is really good. And we do fun science projects in that class.

I also have a history class and we read 100 pages every night! There are only 18 students. It's a (4)_____ , so we talk a lot! That makes me nervous. You know, I don't like to talk in class. But the professor is really nice.

Okay, I have a lot of reading right now! Call me later.

Aleksandra

REAL-WORLD APPLICATION

5 Work with a partner. Find a class schedule at your college.

6 Choose one class. Find this information:

The name of the class is (1)_____ . It meets on (2)_____ (days). It meets in (3)_____ (classroom).

There *is / is not* a quiz section. There *is / is not* a lab class. The class has (4)_____ (number) students.

7 Report to your class. Write the name of the class on the board. Then talk about the class.

8 Discuss the classes. Which one is your favorite? Why?

LEARNING OBJECTIVES

Reading skill	Take notes
Grammar	Subject-verb agreement; determiners: *a*, *an*, and *some*
Academic writing skill	Concluding sentences
Writing Task	Write paragraphs about food in your country
On Campus	Make notes in a text

FOOD AND CULTURE

ACTIVATE YOUR KNOWLEDGE

Work with a partner. Ask and answer the questions.

1 What is the woman doing?
2 What foods do you see?
3 What foods do you usually buy?

WATCH AND LISTEN

Arreau

PREPARING TO WATCH

ACTIVATING YOUR KNOWLEDGE

1 Work with a partner and answer the questions.

1 What kinds of food come from cows? Which ones do you like?
2 What food is popular in your country?
3 Does your country have a national dish? Describe it.

PREDICTING CONTENT USING VISUALS

2 Look at the pictures from the video. Complete the sentences with the words in the box.

> village   farm   fruit   cheese

1 This is a French _____ .
2 Farmers are selling _____ .
3 The goats live on a _____ .
4 The man is making _____ .

GLOSSARY

market (n) a place where people go to buy or sell things

quart (n) a unit of measuring liquid, like milk; 1 quart = 0.95 liters

ingredient (n) one of the different foods that a particular type of food or dish is made from

turn over (phr v) to move something around so that it faces a different direction

WHILE WATCHING

3 ▶ Watch the video. Check (✔) the true statements.

1. ☐ The village of Arreau is in the south of France.
2. ☐ The south of France is very rainy.
3. ☐ Cheese is very popular in France.
4. ☐ People can learn how to make cheese at the Tuchans' farm.
5. ☐ They get milk from the goats once a day.
6. ☐ Salt is one of the ingredients in the cheese.
7. ☐ Mrs. Tuchan makes the cheese, and Mr. Tuchan sells it.

UNDERSTANDING MAIN IDEAS

4 ▶ Watch again. Answer the questions.

1. What do farmers sell in the market? _____
2. What does Mrs. Tuchan sell? _____
3. Where do the goats wait? _____
4. How much milk can a goat make every day? _____
5. Where does Mr. Tuchan put the cheese? _____
6. How long does the cheese stay in the room? _____

UNDERSTANDING DETAILS

5 Match the sentence halves.

1. The farmers have to
2. Making cheese
3. Most French people
4. Most countries

a. like cheese.
b. have traditional foods.
c. take care of the goats.
d. takes time.

MAKING INFERENCES

DISCUSSION

6 Work with a partner and answer the questions.

1. What do you think is interesting or surprising about making goat cheese?
2. What kinds of food or other things can you buy in outdoor markets in your country?
3. Why are traditional foods important?

READING

PREPARING TO READ

1 Ask and answer the questions with a partner.

1 What foods are popular all over the world?
2 Why do you think those foods are popular?
3 What are your favorite foods? Why?

2 You are going to read an article about tea. Read the sentences. Write the words in bold next to the definitions.

1 I enjoy a cup of hot tea in the afternoon. I add **honey** to make it sweet.
2 I play many **different** sports. I am on the soccer, basketball, and tennis teams.
3 My father **prepares** our family's dinner on weekends. He really likes cooking.
4 We buy our **bread** at a bakery. I enjoy it with butter and jam.
5 I have the **same** color eyes as my mother. They are dark gray.
6 There are five main **types** of food: grains, meats, fruits, vegetables, and dairy.
7 When it is hot outside, it is good to have water or other **drinks**.

a _____ (n) a basic food made from flour, water, and salt mixed together and baked
b _____ (adj) like something else
c _____ (adj) not like other things
d _____ (n) something that is part of a group of things that are like each other
e _____ (n) a sweet and sticky food made by bees
f _____ (n) a liquid that you drink, for example, water or soda
g _____ (v) to make something

WHILE READING

3 Read the article. Match each main idea to the correct paragraph. Write the number from the text.

_____ a People use special kettles to prepare tea.
_____ b The history of tea started a long time ago.
_____ c There are different kinds of tea made from tea leaves.
_____ d In Kuala Lumpur, pulled tea is special.
_____ e Tea is very popular.

Tea: A World History

by A. Capper

INTRODUCTION: THE WORLD IN A TEACUP

1 Tea is tasty and good for you. It is also one of the most popular **drinks** around the world. But what is tea? And why is it so popular?

2 All tea comes from tea leaves, but tea is not always the **same**. There are many kinds of tea. You can drink black tea, green tea, white tea, or fruit tea. Each **type** of tea has a **different** taste and a different color.

1.1 A tea seller prepares tea in Kuala Lumpur.

3 The history of tea begins in Asia. In China, Korea, and Japan, tea is still very important today. In Japan, it can take many hours to **prepare** and drink tea with your guests. In Malaysia, a popular drink at breakfast is *teh tarik* ("pulled tea"). Malaysians say it is good for you and tastes good with *roti canai* – a kind of **bread**.

4 Tourists in Kuala Lumpur like watching the tea sellers make "pulled tea." The tea sellers pour hot water on black tea. After five minutes, they add sugar and milk. Then they "pull" the tea – they pour the tea from one cup to another many times.

5 In many countries, you must have a special kettle[1] to make tea. People in different countries also like to add different things to their tea. For example, Russians use a special kettle called a *samovar*. They like drinking tea with lemon. Sometimes, they also drink tea with some sugar or jam. This makes it sweet.

1.2 A Russian samovar

6 In Turkey, tea comes in a *Çaydanlık*. A *Çaydanlık* has two kettles: one for the water and one for the tea. Drink Turkish tea with some sugar.

7 Arab tea, called *karak*, is made with cardamom[2], ginger, milk, and sugar. In the United Kingdom, they add some milk and sugar. In the United States, tea is popular with **honey**.

8 The British usually eat cookies with their tea. In Japan, they like …

[1]**kettle** (n) a container with a lid and a handle for boiling water
[2]**cardamom** (n) a South Asian plant with seeds used as a spice

1.3 A Turkish Çaydanlık set

Taking notes

When you take notes, you write down the important information from the text. You do not need to write complete sentences. Use a chart or outline to organize your ideas.

READING FOR DETAILS

4 Write information from the text in the chart.

country	How is the tea prepared? What do people eat with it?
Malaysia	1 Pour hot water on black tea. • After five minutes, add sugar and milk. • Then "pull" the tea. (Pour the tea from one cup to another many times.) • Eat *roti canai* with it.
Russia	2
Turkey	3
Arab countries	4
United Kingdom	5

SCANNING TO FIND INFORMATION

5 Scan the text. Write the names of the correct countries from the text in the blanks.

1 People in _____ drink *teh tarik*.
2 In _____ , people prepare tea in a *samovar*.
3 People prepare tea for many hours in _____ .
4 Some people in _____ drink tea with sugar or jam.
5 People prepare tea with two kettles in _____ .
6 Tourists like watching tea sellers prepare tea in _____ .

DISCUSSION

6 Work with a partner. Ask and answer the questions.

1 Do you prefer tea or coffee? Why?
2 How do people drink tea in your country? (With sugar? With milk?)
3 Why do you think people drink tea in so many countries?

PREPARING TO READ

USING YOUR KNOWLEDGE

1 Work with a partner. Write different types of foods in the chart and take turns describing them.

What foods do you like to eat in restaurants?	What foods do you like from your country?	What foods do you like from other countries?

2 You are going to read a web article. Look at the text and the photos on page 154. Circle the correct options.

   1 The text is from a website for *tourists / students*.

   2 The text is about different *types of food / things to do* in Melbourne.

3 Read the sentences. Match the words in bold to the photos.

UNDERSTANDING KEY VOCABULARY

PRISM Online Workbook

   1 I eat **meat** for dinner. I like burgers or steak. _____

   2 The restaurant always **serves** tea **with** a cookie. _____

   3 I buy **vegetables** at the market in my city. _____

   4 My dad is a fisherman, so we eat a lot of **fish**. _____

   5 A popular **dish** for breakfast in the United States is pancakes. _____

   6 In Mexico, beans and **rice** are popular. _____

   7 I eat three **meals** a day: breakfast, lunch, and dinner. _____

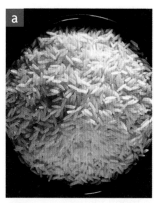

Melbourne/Student Guide

Home | The city | Map | Public transportation | Culture | Entertainment | Help

VOTED THE BEST ONLINE CITY GUIDE BY STUDY AUSTRALIA

10 OF THE BEST BY CUISINE[1]

Arab cuisine

Australian cuisine

American cuisine

Cambodian cuisine

Chinese cuisine

French cuisine

Japanese cuisine

Korean cuisine

Mexican cuisine

Turkish cuisine

Melbourne is a big city. We have cuisines from all over the world. Try some!

kabsa

crocodile

amok trey

Arab cuisine

1   At an Arab restaurant, you can find delicious **meat dishes**. Two popular dishes are *shawarma* and *kabsa*. *Shawarma* is a savory[2] meat dish. The meat is served in *pita* bread with **vegetables**. *Kabsa* is a popular **meal** in many Middle Eastern countries, but it is very popular in Saudi Arabia. *Kabsa* is a dish with **rice**, meat, and vegetables. There are many different ways to prepare *kabsa*. If you like meat dishes, you will enjoy your meal at an Arab restaurant.

2   In addition to the many flavorful meat dishes, Arab cuisine has many delicious vegetable dishes. *Falafel* is ...

Read more ◗

Australian cuisine

3   If you are in Australia, you must try a crocodile or kangaroo dish! Many Australian restaurants serve crocodile curry. Crocodile meat is tasty and very good for you. (It is better that you eat crocodile than a crocodile eats you!) Kangaroo meat is also good for you. Kangaroo burgers are served on a type of bread. Australian restaurants also serve great fish and many other dishes ...

Read more ◗

Cambodian cuisine

4   At a Cambodian restaurant, there are many types of dishes. Cambodians like **fish** with rice. Cambodian dishes are **served with** a lot of vegetables. They are very popular in Cambodian cuisine. One famous dish is *amok trey*. Cambodians prepare *amok trey* with fish, nuts, coconut milk, and egg. There are many tasty dishes, but this is one of the best.

Read more ◗

5   Another dish is ...

[1]**cuisine** (n) a style of cooking
[2]**savory** (adj) food that is salty or spicy and not sweet

WHILE READING

4 Scan the text. Write *T* (true) or *F* (false) next to the statements. Correct any false statements.

SCANNING TO FIND INFORMATION

_____ 1 The different cuisines are in alphabetical order.

_____

_____ 2 *Shawarma* is a fish dish.

_____

_____ 3 *Amok trey* is an Australian dish.

_____

_____ 4 Kangaroo meat is popular in Australian restaurants.

_____

_____ 5 Meat is popular in Arab cuisine.

_____

_____ 6 There are different types of *kabsa*.

_____

_____ 7 Kangaroo burgers are served in a pita.

_____

5 Read the questions. Underline the key words in the text. Then write the answers to the questions.

READING FOR DETAILS

1 Where is *kabsa* a very popular dish?

_____

2 Which dishes are served in or on bread?

_____

3 Which kinds of meat are good for you?

_____

4 Which cuisines have rice dishes?

_____

5 Which cuisines have fish dishes?

_____

DISCUSSION

6 Work with a partner. Ask and answer the questions.

1 What type of food can you get in all the cuisines in Reading 2 on page 154?

2 What dishes do you want to try from Reading 2? Why?

3 Use information from Reading 1 and Reading 2 to answer the following question: Why do different countries have special ways of preparing food and drinks?

⊙ LANGUAGE DEVELOPMENT

VOCABULARY ABOUT FOOD

PRISM Online Workbook

1 Choose the word or phrase that has the same meaning as the word in bold.

1 Tea is a **popular** drink all over the world.
   a well liked
   b interesting

2 *Amok trey* is a **tasty** dish from Cambodia.
   a nice
   b fish

3 *Amok trey* is **made with** fish, nuts, coconut milk, and egg.
   a prepared with
   b tastes like

4 Sugar makes tea taste **sweet**.
   a delicious, like honey
   b salty

5 *Shawarma* is **served in** pita bread.
   a comes inside
   b tastes like

6 In Great Britain, tea is often **served with** cookies.
   a cooked with
   b comes with

7 Meat dishes are **savory**.
   a sweet and sugary
   b salty and spicy

8 Fish is **good for** you. People who eat fish live longer.
   a has a good effect on your body
   b tastes good and sweet to you

9 Some people don't like **spicy** food. The taste is too strong and hot.
   a with strong flavors from spices, like cardamom, ginger, chili, etc.
   b food that is hard to bite and eat

2 Work with a partner and list dishes for each word or phrase. Use your own ideas and look at the pictures from Exercise 3 on page 153 and from Reading 2 to help you.

description	dishes
sweet	
savory	
good for you	
tasty	
popular	
spicy	

3 Look at the foods you have listed. With a partner, discuss how they are prepared and what they are usually served with.

COUNT AND NONCOUNT NOUNS

Count nouns name things you can count, such as vegetables, drinks, and meals. They can have a singular or a plural form and a singular or a plural verb.

singular	plural
One **vegetable is** cabbage.	**Vegetables are** served in *pita* bread.
A popular **dish is** *shawarma*.	Two popular **dishes are** *shawarma* and *kabsa*.

Noncount nouns have a singular form and a singular verb. They do not have a plural form or a verb.

Fish is good for you. ~~Fishes are good for you~~.
Rice is served with many Indian dishes. ~~Rices are served with many Indian dishes~~.

PRISM Online Workbook

4 Read the sentences. Check (✔) if they are correct and cross out (✗) if they are wrong. Use a dictionary to help you.

_____ 1 Honeys are sweet.
_____ 2 Vegetables are popular in European cuisine.
_____ 3 Milks are good for children.
_____ 4 Bread are tasty.
_____ 5 Cookies are served with tea.
_____ 6 Burgers are served on a type of bread.
_____ 7 Fish are good for you.
_____ 8 Waters are served in a glass.

5 Correct the wrong sentences in Exercise 4.

_____

_____

_____

_____

_____

WRITING

CRITICAL THINKING

At the end of this unit, you are going to do the Writing Task below.

> Write about popular food in your country.

SKILLS

Brainstorming

If you plan or create ideas in a group, you are *brainstorming*. You can work in groups to create a list of words about a topic.

1 Work with a partner. Write words to describe the dish in the idea map. Explain what it is made of, tastes like, and is served with. Look at Reading 2 on page 154 to help you.

UNDERSTAND ▲

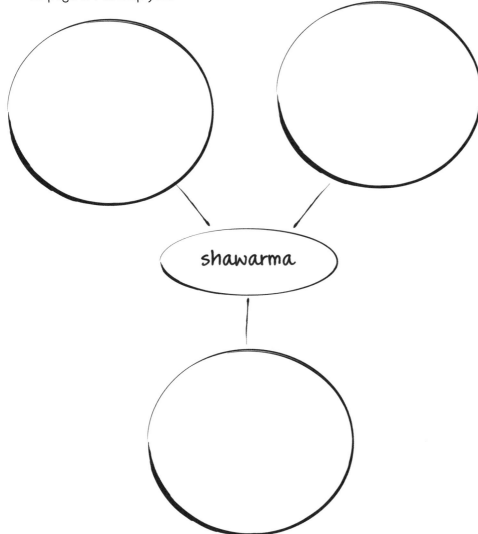

shawarma

2 Work in small groups. Brainstorm and list popular dishes from your country.

_____

_____

_____

_____

3 Choose two popular dishes from Exercise 2. Write the name of the dish in the middle of each idea map. Brainstorm words to explain what each dish is made of, tastes like, and is served with.

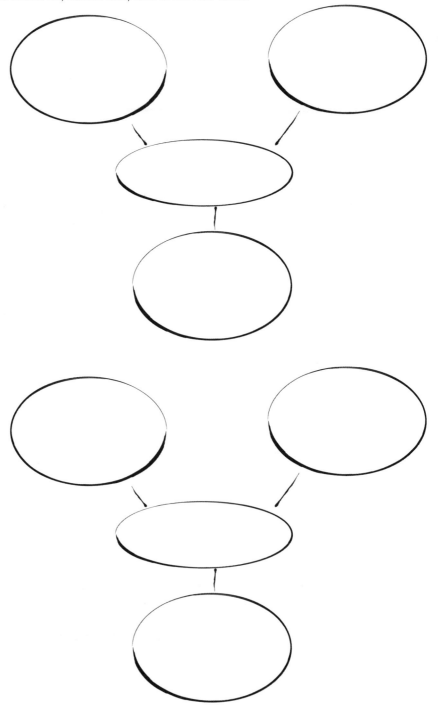

GRAMMAR FOR WRITING

SUBJECT–VERB AGREEMENT

A sentence must have a *subject* and a *verb*. The subject can be singular or plural. The verb must agree with the subject.

Use a singular verb form with a singular subject.

subject   verb
This **dish**   **is** tasty.

subject   verb
It   **is** a popular dish.

subject   verb
Vietnamese cuisine   **uses** coconut milk.

Use a plural verb form with a plural subject.

subject   verb
The **dishes**   **are** tasty.

subject   verb
They   **are** popular dishes.

subject   verb
Some people   **like** spicy food.

Remember: Noncount nouns must have a singular verb form. See Language Development on page 158.

1 Circle the correct verb forms.

1 Turkish chefs *prepare / prepares* small dishes called *meze*.
2 Latin American cuisine *use / uses* a lot of vegetables.
3 A famous dish in Japan *is / are* sushi.
4 Rice *is / are* popular in many restaurants in Korea.
5 Chinese food *is / are* served with rice and vegetables.
6 Two popular rice dishes in Thailand *is / are* called *khao mok kai* and *khao na pet*.

PRISM Online Workbook

2 Read the sentences. Check (✔) if they are correct and cross out (✘) if they are wrong. Use a dictionary to help you.

_____ 1 Korean restaurants serves rice with meat and vegetables.

_____ 2 Butter is served with bread.

_____ 3 Latin American chefs uses many different kinds of vegetables in their dishes.

_____ 4 Hamburgers is served on a type of bread.

_____ 5 Apples and bananas are sweet.

_____ 6 French vegetable soup are delicious.

3 Correct the wrong sentences in Exercise 2.

_____

_____

_____

_____

_____

DETERMINERS: *A, AN,* AND *SOME*

LANGUAGE

Articles are *a, an, the,* and "no article." Write articles before a noun or noun phrase.

Use the articles *a* or *an* before a singular count noun. Use *a* before a consonant sound. Use *an* before a vowel sound.

A famous dish from Italy is risotto. Amok trey is **a** popular Cambodian dish. Jambalaya is **an** American dish. **An apple** is served with this dish.

Do not use *a / an* before a noncount noun.

~~Add a honey to the dish. English people drink tea with a milk.~~

Add honey to the dish. English people drink tea with milk.

You can use *some* before:

• a plural count noun (vegetables, drinks)

• a noncount noun (milk, rice)

Some means "more than one" before a count noun.

Some cookies are served with the coffee. Chefs prepare the dish with **some vegetables**.

Some means "a (small) part of" before a noncount noun.

Add **some honey** to the dish. English people drink tea with **some milk**.

4 Correct the underlined parts of the sentences.

1 At <u>some Arab restaurant,</u> you can find delicious meat dishes.

_____

2 The curry is served with <u>a rice</u>.

_____

3 <u>Some famous dish</u> in New Orleans <u>is</u> *jambalaya* and *gumbo*.

_____

4 French chefs add <u>a apple</u> to this dish.

_____

5 Korean chefs prepare many dishes with <u>a meat</u>.

_____

6 <u>Australian</u> like eating <u>a crocodile meat</u>.

_____

7 There are <u>some vegetable</u> in Korean *kimchi*.

_____

8 <u>Some popular dish</u> in Latin America is chicken soup.

_____

CONCLUDING SENTENCES

SKILLS

A *concluding sentence* ends a paragraph. Often it repeats the main idea of the paragraph using different words.

topic sentence + supporting sentences

All tea comes from tea leaves, but tea is not always the same. There are many kinds of tea. You can drink black tea, green tea, white tea, or fruit tea.

concluding sentence

Each type of tea has a different taste and a different color.

In the example above, the last sentence is the concluding sentence. It repeats the main idea that tea is not always the same.

 PRISM Online Workbook

1 Read the first sentence of a paragraph. Then check (✔) the concluding sentence.

1 At a Cambodian restaurant, there are many types of dishes.
_____ One famous dish is *amok trey*.
_____ Cambodians prepare *amok trey* with fish, nuts, coconut milk, and egg.
_____ There are many tasty dishes, but this is one of the best.
_____ The coconut milk makes it sweet.

2 At an Arab restaurant, you can find delicious meat dishes.
_____ *Shawarma* is a savory meat dish.
_____ *Kabsa* is a dish with rice, meat, and vegetables.
_____ If you like tasty meat dishes, you will enjoy your meal at an Arab restaurant.
_____ *Kabsa* is a popular meal in many Middle Eastern countries, but it is very popular in Saudi Arabia.

2 Read the paragraphs. Then write a concluding sentence.

1   France is known for its great bakeries. You can get delicious bread, cookies, and other sweet food at these stores. The French are also known for their tasty cheeses. A popular meal is bread and cheese.

_____

_____

2   Brazilian restaurants serve delicious meat dishes. The meat is cooked over a fire and salted. It is often served with vegetables. You can find this savory dish at most restaurants.

_____

_____

Write about popular food in your country.

PLAN

1 Look at the brainstorming notes you made in Critical Thinking.

2 Think of any more information you would like to add to your paragraphs.

WRITE A FIRST DRAFT

3 Follow the directions to write a paragraph about each dish. Refer to the Task Checklist as you prepare your paragraphs.

   1 Say what dishes are popular in your country.
   2 Describe the taste of the first dish. Describe what the dish is made of. Explain what the dish is served in or served with.
   3 Describe the taste of the second dish. Describe what the dish is made of. Tell what the dish is served in or served with.

4 Write a concluding sentence to each paragraph.

EDIT

5 Now use the Task Checklist to edit your paragraphs.

TASK CHECKLIST	✔
Write a paragraph about each dish.	
Make sure subjects and verbs agree in your sentences.	
Use the article *a / an* before a singular count noun.	
Use *some* before a plural count noun or a noncount noun.	
End each paragraph with a concluding sentence.	

6 Make any necessary changes to your paragraphs.

ON CAMPUS

MAKING NOTES IN A TEXT

Remembering important information

Good students annotate and make notes in their books. Annotation means underlining, circling, and highlighting words. This helps students remember the main ideas and find important information quickly.

PREPARING TO READ

1 Work with a partner. Discuss the questions.

  1 Do you annotate your textbooks? How?
  2 Do you make notes in your textbooks? What do you write?
  3 How do you use your annotations and notes?

WHILE READING

2 Read the handout about annotating and making notes.

A Tips for Annotating and Making Notes

1. Highlight the important ideas. Do not highlight everything!

2. Circle new vocabulary words.

3. Underline definitions and examples.

4. Write your ideas and questions in the margin. Use a pencil.

5. Use abbreviations. Use your own abbreviations, too.

abbreviation	meaning
ex.	example
def.	definition

6. Don't write in library books.

B Sample

Food is different around the world. One difference is in staple foods. Every culture has a staple food. A staple is a basic food in most meals. For example, in Asia, rice is a staple. In Germany, the staple is potatoes, but in Morocco, coucous is the staple. In most countries the staple is a starch.

def.

corn in my country?

ex.

3 Read Part A of the handout again. Write *T* (true) or *F* (false) next to the statements below.

_____ 1 I should write my own ideas and questions in my book.

_____ 2 I can write in a book from the library.

_____ 3 I can use my own abbreviations in my book.

_____ 4 I should highlight all the words in a paragraph.

4 Match the two columns. Use the examples in Part B of the handout to help you.

1 One difference is in staple foods.   a a new vocabulary word
2 A staple is a basic food in most meals.   b her own question
3 in Asia, rice is a staple   c an important idea
4 corn in my country?   d an example
5 starch   e a definition

PRACTICE

5 Make notes in the paragraph below.

1 Highlight an important idea.
2 Underline an example and make a note about it.
3 Underline a definition and make a note about it.
4 Circle a new vocabulary word.
5 Write your own question or idea about the paragraph in the margin.
6 Share your annotations and notes with a partner.

People in different cultures also eat different foods for breakfast. In the U.S., many people have oatmeal. Some Americans like to eat eggs and bacon. In Japan, they eat fish for breakfast. In Turkey, they have olives, bread, and feta. Feta is a white, salty cheese.

REAL-WORLD APPLICATION

6 Work with a partner.

1 Choose one paragraph from one of your textbooks.
2 Make annotations and notes in the paragraph.
3 Discuss your work with your partner.

LEARNING OBJECTIVES

Reading Skill	Skim a text
Grammar	Subject–verb–object; link sentences with pronouns
Academic writing skill	Give reasons with *because* and results with *so*
Writing Task	Write a paragraph about a transportation survey
On Campus	Get to campus and around town

TRANSPORTATION

ACTIVATE YOUR KNOWLEDGE

Work with a partner. Ask and answer the questions.

1 How do people in this city get to work and school?
2 Which way looks the fastest? Why?
3 How do you travel to get to work and school? Why?

WATCH AND LISTEN

PREPARING TO WATCH

ACTIVATING YOUR KNOWLEDGE

1 Work with a partner and answer the questions.

1 What are the most common types of transportation in your city?
2 What are some unusual types of transportation?
3 What cities have subway systems?

PREDICTING CONTENT USING VISUALS

2 Look at the pictures from the video. Circle the correct word.

1 This train is *underground / over ground*.
2 Many people are waiting to get *on / off* the train.
3 The city is *busy / quiet*.
4 The man is helping people in the *shopping mall / subway station*.

GLOSSARY

rider (n) a person who rides in a car, train, or bus, or on a bike or motorcycle

platform (n) the area in a train or subway station where you get on and off a train

attendant (n) someone whose job is to help people in a particular place

calm (adj) relaxed; not worried or excited

WHILE WATCHING

UNDERSTANDING MAIN IDEAS

3 ▶ Watch the video. Write *T* (true) or *F* (false) next to the statements. Correct the false statements.

_____ 1 Every day, millions of people travel on subways that are under the ground.
_____ 2 The oldest subway system is in Tokyo.
_____ 3 London's subway system is called the "Tube."
_____ 4 London has the busiest subway system.
_____ 5 Attendants help keep riders safe, calm, and on time.

4 ▶ Watch again. Choose the correct answer.

   1 How many subway systems are in the world today?

      a over 500

      b over 250

      c over 150

   2 How do 500,000 Londoners get to work each day?

      a They go by subway.

      b They walk.

      c They drive.

   3 How many people take the Tokyo subway system every hour?

      a 3,500

      b 35,000

      c 350,000

   4 Which statement is <u>not</u> true about Tokyo?

      a There are more people in Tokyo than any other city.

      b There are no subway attendants.

      c There are 8 million riders on Tokyo's subway every day.

5 Complete the sentences with the words in the box.

> faster   helpful   traffic   usually

   1 There is less _____ on the streets when people take the subway.

   2 If you work in a city, subways are often _____ than cars.

   3 People in Tokyo are _____ on time for work.

   4 It is _____ to have an attendant on the subway platform.

DISCUSSION

6 Work with a partner and answer the questions.

   1 Have you traveled on the subway in London, Tokyo, New York City, or another large city? How was it?

   2 Subways help people in cities like London and Tokyo get to work. What are some other benefits of subways to cities?

   3 What do you think are the most convenient ways to travel in a city? Why?

READING

PREPARING TO READ

PREVIEWING

1 You are going to read about transportation. Work with a partner. Look at the text on page 173 and answer the questions.

1 What type of text is this?
2 Why do people write this type of text?

UNDERSTANDING
KEY VOCABULARY

2 Read the sentences. Choose the best definition for the word or phrase in bold.

1 The **traffic** is moving slowly. There are a lot of cars on the road.
   a the cars, trucks, etc., driving on the road
   b the time it takes to get somewhere

2 When does the **train** get into the station? I need to be there by 9 a.m.
   a a long, thin type of car that travels on tracks with people or things
   b a route or way for traveling from one place to another

3 I take the **subway** to work. I only have to go two stops.
   a a place for people to walk along the road
   b trains that travel underground, usually in a city

4 Many children learn to ride **bikes**. It's a fun and easy way to travel.
   a a type of transportation with two wheels that you sit on and move by turning two pedals
   b a type of transportation with four wheels and an engine.

5 I paid a **taxi** driver to take me from the airport to the city.
   a a place for planes to land and people to get on planes
   b a car with a driver who you pay to take you somewhere

6 My son takes the **bus** to school with other kids from his class.
   a a big type of car that takes many people around a city
   b a small car with three wheels

7 People don't ride **motorcycles** where I live. It is rainy, and they don't want to get wet.
   a a big bike with an engine for one or two people
   b railway tracks for moving things

8 In cities, there are many **transportation** choices. You can take a bus, subway, car, or bike to work.
   a the things people use to move themselves or things from one place to another
   b the people living in a certain area

We are a group of engineering students from Canada. This summer, we are studying at Bangkok University of Science and Technology (BUST). We would like to find out:

1 how people in Bangkok travel.
2 how people feel about **transportation** in Bangkok.

Please answer the questions below. Answering the questions takes about five minutes.

Check (✔) the correct boxes to answer the questions.

A. About you

A1 How old are you?
- ☐ 14–17
- ☐ 18–21
- ☐ 22–31
- ☑ 32–53
- ☐ older than 53

A2 I am: ☐ male ☑ female

A3 What do you do?
- ☐ study
- ☑ work

B. Travel

B1 How long is your trip to work or school?
- ☐ 5–15 minutes
- ☑ 15–45 minutes
- ☐ 45–60 minutes
- ☐ more than 1 hour

B2 How do you get to work or school?
- ☐ on foot[2]
- ☐ **bike**
- ☐ car
- ☐ tuk-tuk
- ☐ **motorcycle**
- ☐ water taxi
- ☐ **taxi**
- ☐ Sky**Train**
- ☑ **subway**
- ☐ **bus**

B3 How often do you use these types of transportation?

Table 1

types of transportation	always	often	sometimes	not often	never
on foot	✓				
bike				✓	
car		✓			
motorcycle					✓
water taxi			✓		
taxi			✓		
bus			✓		
SkyTrain			✓		
subway		✓			

B4 Which type or types of transportation do you own?
I own a: ☐ bike ☑ car ☐ motorcycle
☐ other (Please write.): _____

C. Opinion

C1 Read the statements in the chart. Do you agree or disagree with them?

Table 2

statements	strongly agree	agree	neither agree nor disagree	disagree	strongly disagree
There is a lot of **traffic** in Bangkok.	✓				
The traffic makes me late.		✓			
We need more public transportation.	✓				

C2 Write any comments or suggestions that you have about transportation in Bangkok.

We should create more subway lines. Then more people could use the subway, and there would not be so much traffic on the roads.

tuk-tuk

SkyTrain

water taxi

[1] **survey** (n) a set of questions people are asked to get information
[2] **on foot** (prep phr) if you go somewhere on foot, you walk there.

Thank you for taking the time to answer the questions in this survey.

READING 1 173

WHILE READING

Skimming a text

Skimming is useful when you want to understand what a text is about. When you skim, you look for the main ideas in a text and ignore the details. Main ideas are usually found at the beginning of paragraphs.

SKIMMING

3 Skim the text. What information is the survey asking about? Circle the correct topics below.

1 the number of hours people in Bangkok work or study
2 how people travel in Bangkok
3 the cost of transportation in Bangkok
4 popular forms of transportation in Bangkok
5 how people in Bangkok travel on vacation
6 what forms of transportation people own

SCANNING TO FIND INFORMATION

4 Scan the text for the survey answers.

1 How old is the person? _____
2 How long is the person's trip? _____
3 How does the person travel to work? _____
4 What does the person never use for transportation? _____
5 Does the person think the traffic makes her late? _____

READING FOR DETAILS

5 Write *T* (true) or *F* (false). Correct the false statements.

_____ 1 There is not a place for people to write their suggestions in the survey.

_____

_____ 2 The survey asks if the person is male or female.

_____

_____ 3 The purpose of the survey is to see how people like Bangkok.

_____

_____ 4 The person answering the survey often takes the bus.

_____

_____ 5 The person answering the survey thinks more water taxis should be added.

_____

DISCUSSION

6 Work with a partner. Ask and answer the questions.

1 What type of transportation do people usually use in your city or town?

2 Which types of transportation are the best and which are the worst for:
   a long trips?   **c** places with no roads?
   b getting in shape and healthy?   **d** families?

READING 2

PREPARING TO READ

USING YOUR
KNOWLEDGE

1 You are going to read a report about transportation in Bangkok. A report is a description of something or information about something. Work with a partner to complete the chart with ideas.

report	information
weather report	information about _____
news report	information about _____
_____	_____

2 Look at the text and the pie chart on page 177. Answer each question by circling the correct option.

1 What type of text is it?
   a a news report
   b a report for a university class
   c an email to the writer's family
2 What is the main topic of this text?
   a weather
   b food
   c transportation
3 Who wrote this text?
   a a student
   b a teacher
   c a journalist

3 Use the words in the box to complete the sentences. Use the correct form. Some sentences have more than one answer.

> **drive** (v) to make a car, bus, or train move by controlling it
> **prefer** (v) to like someone or something more than another person or thing
> **report** (n) information about an event or situation
> **result** (n) information that you get from something, like an exam, a survey, a medical test, etc.
> **ride** (v) to travel by sitting in a car or train or on a bike
> **spend** (v) to use time by doing something
> **take** (v) to travel somewhere using a car, bus, or train

1 I _____ riding my bike to riding in a car. I like to be outside.
2 My mom _____ the bus to work every day. She gets there in ten minutes.
3 My dad _____ 40 minutes in traffic every morning. Driving in the morning takes a lot of time.
4 The traffic _____ said that traffic was moving slowly all over the city.
5 I got the _____ back from my test. I did great!
6 The bus driver _____ too fast! He should go more slowly on these busy streets.
7 I _____ the subway into the city on the weekends. It's nice not to drive.

4 Scan the text. Write the correct numbers in the blanks on the pie chart (Figure 1).

Student Name: **Simon Lancaster**
Student ID: **100035478 / Bangkok University of Science and Technology**
Course: **Transportation and the City**

Transportation in Bangkok: Report

1   This **report** shows the **results** of a survey about transportation in Bangkok. Over eight million people live in the city. The pie chart (Figure 1) shows the most popular types of transportation in Bangkok. It shows the percentage[1] of people who use each type of transportation to get to work or school.

2   Every day, thousands of people use public and private transportation. A popular form of public transportation is the SkyTrain. People take public transportation so they don't have to drive themselves. Twenty-one percent of the population of Bangkok takes the SkyTrain to work or school. Another form of public transportation in the city is the bus. Eighteen percent of people who live in Bangkok **take** buses. People **prefer** buses to tuk-tuks because buses cost less money. Only 8% of people use tuk-tuks to get to work or school. Most people in Bangkok use private transportation. They **drive** their own cars. Fourteen percent of people **ride** motorcycles to get to work or take children to school. Only 3% walk to work, and only 2% bike to work. Most places of work are too far away to walk or bike to.

3   There is a lot of traffic in Bangkok. The roads are full of different types of vehicles[2] (cars, motorcycles, tuk-tuks, etc.). Twenty-three percent of people drive a car to work or school. Most people **spend** more than one hour every day traveling because the traffic is so bad. Almost 35% of people are late because of traffic jams. However, there are no traffic jams on the river. Eleven percent of people take the water taxi.

[1]**percentage** (n) how many out of 100
[2]**vehicles** (n) things such as cars or buses that take people from one place to another, especially using roads

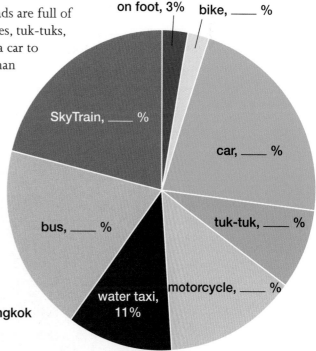

Figure 1: Means of transportation in Bangkok by popularity

5 Write the words and phrases from the box in the blanks. You can use a word more than once. You may have to change verb form.

| drive   motorcycles   take   traffic   transportation |

This report shows the results of a survey about ⁽¹⁾_____ in Bangkok. Over eight million people live in Bangkok. The pie chart (Figure 1) shows the most popular types of transportation in Bangkok. It shows the percentage of people who use each type of transportation to get to work or school. Twenty-one percent of the population of Bangkok ⁽²⁾_____ the SkyTrain to work or school. Another way to travel is to ⁽³⁾_____ the bus. However, it is more popular to ⁽⁴⁾_____ your own car. There is a lot of ⁽⁵⁾_____ in Bangkok. The roads are full of cars, ⁽⁶⁾_____ , etc.

6 Read the text again. Underline the information that answers each question and write it below.

1 How many people live in Bangkok?

_____

2 Is the SkyTrain a public or private form of transportation?

_____

3 What percentage of people drive cars?

_____

4 How long do most people spend in traffic?

_____

5 What percentage of people are late because of traffic jams?

_____

DISCUSSION

7 Work with a partner. Ask and answer the questions.

1 What is the most popular way to get to work in Bangkok? Why do you think that is?

2 If you lived in Bangkok, what transportation would you use? Why?

3 Use information from Reading 1 and Reading 2 to answer the questions: Why is it important for cities to know how people get to work? Which type of transportation do you think is best for cities? Why?

⊙ LANGUAGE DEVELOPMENT

QUANTIFIERS

Quantifiers tell you the answer to the question *How many?* Use quantifiers before a noun. For small numbers, use *a few*, *not many*, and *some*. For bigger numbers, use *many*, *a lot of*, and *most*.

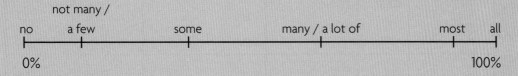

There are **a lot of taxis** in New York.
A few people take tuk-tuks in Bangkok.
Not many people take taxis in Tokyo.
Some trains are very fast.
Many people work downtown.
Most people in Bangkok drive their own cars.

1 Read the sentences. Circle the quantifiers and underline the nouns the quantifiers refer to.

PRISM Online Workbook

1 Most people in Bangkok drive their own cars.
2 Some people ride motorcycles.
3 Not many people bike to work or school.
4 A few people take the water taxi.
5 Many people take the SkyTrain.

2 Read the sentences and write quantifiers in the blanks. Use the percentages to help you. More than one answer is possible.

1 _____ (62%) people in London take the subway to work.

2 _____ (8%) people drive their cars to work in London.

3 Today, _____ (18%) people in London bike to work.

4 _____ (9%) people in London take the bus to work.

5 _____ (3%) people in London walk or run to work.

TRANSPORTATION COLLOCATIONS

LANGUAGE

You can use these types of collocations when you talk about transportation.

subject	verb	determiner	noun (transportation)	prepositional phrase (to + place)
Many students People	take	the their a	bus subway cars taxi	to school. to work.
My parents	drive	their a	car	to work.
I	ride	the a	bus subway bike motorcycle	to school.

subject	verb	prepositional phrase (to + place)	prepositional phrase (by + noun for transportation)
Many students People	travel get	to school to work	by bus. by subway. by car.

3 Put the words in order to make sentences.

1 to / take / school / We / a bus / .

_____

2 travels / by / work / train / Melissa / to / .

_____

3 takes / to / the city / his car / Shu / .

_____

4 get to / work / Many people / motorcycle / by / .

_____

5 by / My children / bike / get to / school / .

_____

6 a taxi / to / the store / Suni / takes / .

_____

4 Read the sentences. Write the correct form of the verbs in the blanks. You can use the words more than once.

drive   ride   take

1 David _____ a motorcycle. His mother does not like it.
2 I _____ a taxi to the airport.
3 Ali can _____ a bike to work.
4 Alison usually _____ the bus to school.
5 Saad prefers to _____ a car.

WRITING

CRITICAL THINKING

At the end of this unit, you are going to do the Writing Task below.

▶ Write about the results of a survey about transportation.

SKILLS

Collecting data

Before you write, you can *collect data*. You can use questionnaires and surveys to collect data.

▲ UNDERSTAND

1 Look back at Reading 2 on page 177. Check (✔) the number of the paragraph or paragraphs that state the percentages in the pie chart.

_____ 1 _____ 2 _____ 3

▲ ANALYZE

2 Now look at the results from a survey on transportation in Chicago. Match the questions to the results.

We asked over one million workers the following questions:

1 Do you use public transportation? If so, what type? _____
2 If you don't use public transportation, how do you get to work? _____
3 Which statements do you agree with? _____

a The bus takes too long. There is too much traffic. The water taxi is not close to my work. It takes too long to walk to my work.
b 17% take the subway or other train. Eight percent take the bus. Two percent ride a water taxi.
c One percent bike to work. Seven percent walk to work. Three percent take a taxi to work. The other 63% drive to work.

3 Underline the information in Exercise 2 that you could show in a pie chart.

▲ CREATE

4 Use the information from Exercise 2. Write the percentages and names of transportation in the pie chart.

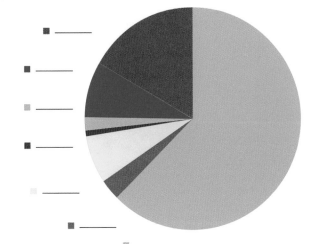

5 With a partner, ask and answer questions about the pie chart.

1 How do most workers in Chicago get to work?
2 How do some workers in Chicago get to work?
3 How do a few workers in Chicago get to work?

6 Discuss the results. Why do you think people use the different types of transportation?

GRAMMAR FOR WRITING

SUBJECT–VERB–OBJECT

LANGUAGE

A sentence is about a *subject*. The subject is a *pronoun*, a *noun*, or a *noun phrase*. The *verb* is after the subject in a sentence. A sentence can have an *object*. The object is a pronoun, a noun, or a noun phrase. The object is after the verb.

subject: **14% of people** ride motorcycles. **11% of people** take the water taxi.

verb: 14% of people **ride** motorcycles. 11% of people **take** the water taxi.

object of verb: 14% of people ride **motorcycles**. 11% of people take **the water taxi**.

A prepositional phrase is <u>not</u> the object of a verb.

	prepositional phrase	*prepositional phrase*
Many students in the class travel	**to school**	**by subway**

	prepositional phrase	*prepositional phrase*
A few students in the class get	**to school**	**by car**.

1 Read the sentences. Check (✔) if the bold word is the object of the verb.

PRISM Online Workbook

_____ 1 Many people travel by **car**.
_____ 2 Many people in Hong Kong take a **water taxi** to work.
_____ 3 Students in Rio de Janeiro do not bike to their **universities**.
_____ 4 In Costa Rica, families often ride **motorcycles** to work and school.
_____ 5 Most people in Moscow travel by **subway**.

2 Read the sentences. Two of the sentences have objects. Find the objects and underline them.

1 Jamila and Kamilah travel to school by car.
2 Juan drives a car to college.
3 Some people walk to work in New York.
4 Many people ride bikes to work in London.
5 People in Bangkok prefer to take the SkyTrain.

3 Work with a partner. Correct the mistakes in the sentences.

1 In Abu Dhabi, cars people drive to work.

_____

2 Not many people in Ankara take to work taxis.

_____

3 Workers in Seoul take the train work.

_____

4 Most students to school motorcycles ride.

_____

5 Some students in Paris take to college the bus.

_____

LINKING SENTENCES WITH PRONOUNS

Use *pronouns* when you do not want to repeat the same noun or noun phrase in a paragraph. The pronouns *he*, *she*, *it*, and *they* can replace nouns. You can use pronouns to link *subjects* or *objects* in different sentences.

subject: **The pie chart** shows the most popular types of transportation in Bangkok. ~~The pie chart~~ **It** shows the percentage of people who use each type of transportation to get to work or school.

object: Many students ride **motorcycles**. ~~Motorcycles~~ **They** are not expensive.

PRISM Online Workbook

4 Match the sentences. Use the words in bold to help you.

1 **Jamila and Kamilah** travel to school by car. _____
2 **Jordan** drives a car to college. _____
3 **Some people** bike to work in New York. _____
4 Many workers ride a **bike** to work in London. _____
5 People in Bangkok prefer to take the **SkyTrain**. _____

a **He** is a good driver.
b **It** is cheaper than a tuk-tuk!
c **It** is a healthy form of transportation.
d **They** travel in their father's car.
e **They** can ride on special roads for bikes.

5 Read the pairs of sentences. Write the correct pronouns in the blanks.

1 Not many workers travel by **taxi**. _____ is an expensive type of transportation.

2 Many people in Hong Kong take the **bus** to work. _____ does not cost much.

3 **Students** in Mexico City do not bike to college. _____ drive there.

4 In Chile, **families** often drive a car to work and school. _____ travel together.

5 Most people in Tokyo travel by **subway**. _____ is the busiest subway system in the world.

ACADEMIC WRITING SKILLS

GIVING REASONS WITH *BECAUSE* AND RESULTS WITH *SO*

Use *because* and *so* to show reasons and results. Sentences with *because* and *so* often have two clauses that each have a subject and a verb. The clause after *because* is the reason clause, and the clause after *so* is the *result* clause.

subject verb   *subject verb*
<u>People</u> <u>prefer</u> buses to tuk-tuks **because** <u>buses</u> <u>cost</u> less money.

subject verb   *subject verb*
<u>People</u> <u>take</u> public transportation **so** <u>they</u> <u>don't have to</u> drive themselves.

Use *because of* to give a reason. A pronoun, noun, or noun phrase comes after *because of*.

                                      noun phrase
Almost 35% of people are late **because of** <u>traffic jams</u>.

1 Match each sentence half.

1 Most people spend more than one hour every day traveling _____

2 Many people travel by water taxi _____

3 Many people bike to work _____

4 Taxis are expensive _____

5 People don't ride motorcycles _____

a so not many people take them.

b because the traffic is so bad.

c so the city made special roads for bikes.

d because of rain.

e because the city is on a river.

2 Complete each sentence. Use your own ideas to give reasons or results.

1 In my city, only a few people walk to work _____ .

2 Many people take the bus or train to school _____ .

3 A few people take taxis to work _____ .

4 Driving a car takes a long time _____ .

WRITING TASK

Write about the results of a survey about transportation.

PLAN

1 Look at the results of the survey and pie chart from Critical Thinking.

2 You are going to use the results to write about transportation in Chicago. Refer to the Task Checklist as you prepare your paragraph.

WRITE A FIRST DRAFT

3 Write your topic sentence first. See Unit 4 for help with paragraph structure.

4 Write sentences to add details about the topic.

1 Write a sentence about the seven forms of transportation in the survey.

2 Write three or four sentences about the percentage of people who use each form of transportation.

3 Write two or three sentences that compare popular forms of transportation in the city.

4 Write two sentences that give reasons why people use the different types of transportation.

5 Write a sentence about the most popular form of transportation in the city.

6 Write a concluding sentence.

5 Put your topic sentence, detail sentences, and concluding sentence together to make a paragraph.

EDIT

6 Use the Task Checklist to edit your paragraph.

TASK CHECKLIST	✔
Use data from the survey on transportation in Chicago.	
Use percentages from your pie chart.	
Write a topic sentence, supporting sentences, and a concluding sentence.	
Use pronoun links in your sentences.	
Use *so* and *because* to give results and reasons.	

7 Make any necessary changes to your paragraph.

ON CAMPUS

GETTING TO CAMPUS AND AROUND TOWN

Transportation

College students need good transportation. They need to get to campus, they need to go shopping, and they also like to go out with friends.

PREPARING TO READ

1 Work with a partner. Discuss the questions.

   1 How do you get to campus?

   2 How do you get around campus?

   3 Which kind of transportation is on your campus?

     ☐ subway   ☐ bus   ☐ train   ☐ Uber

     ☐ bike rental   ☐ carpool program   ☐ campus shuttle bus

   4 Do you use public transportation? Is it difficult to use?

   5 Do you have a driver's license? Why / Why not?

WHILE READING

2 Read about three students and their transportation choices.

Petra

I take public transportation everywhere. I get to campus by bus. I have a student bus pass, so it's cheap. Sometimes it's not easy, for example, when I have a lot of groceries. Also, I don't like to take it late at night.

Marco

I love my bike. I ride it all over the city. Sometimes there's a lot of traffic. Then my bike is faster than a car. It's also good for riding around campus. Riding my bike is good exercise, but it's not very much fun in the rain. Also, I can't go to the mountains or ski area by bike. I need a car for that.

Ahmed

I get to school by car. My friends and I carpool together in the mornings. A car is very convenient, but it's also very expensive. For example, I have to pay for insurance, parking, and my driver's license. I also need gas.

3 Choose the correct answer to complete each sentence.

   1 Petra rides the bus because _____ .

     a it's easy   **b** she likes to ride at night

     c it's cheap with a student bus pass

   2 Marco enjoys his bicycle because _____ .

     a it's faster than a car   **b** he rides to the ski area

     c he likes to ride in the rain

   3 Sometimes Ahmed doesn't like having a car because _____ .

     a it's convenient   **b** his friends ride with him

     c he has to pay for a lot of things

4 Write *T* (true) or *F* (false) next to the statements.

   _____ **1** Riding a bike is good for you.

   _____ **2** Ahmed and his friends ride to school together.

   _____ **3** Petra likes to go shopping for food by bus.

   _____ **4** Marco often rides his bike to the mountains.

   _____ **5** Ahmed needs to pay for his driver's license.

   _____ **6** Petra enjoys the bus at night.

PRACTICE

5 Complete the sentences below. Make the sentences true for you.

Every day, I get to class (1)_____ (how?). I like this type
of transportation because (2)_____ (why?). Sometimes,
I don't like this transportation because (3)_____ (why?).
After class, I often go (4)_____ (where?). I get there
(5)_____ (how?). It takes about (6)_____
(how many?) minutes.

REAL-WORLD APPLICATION

6 Work with a partner. Choose your favorite type of transportation in your
town or city.

   a Why do you like it?

   b What don't you like?

   c When do you use it and where do you go?

7 Make a brochure about your favorite type of transportation. Include the
information from Exercise 6.

8 Share your brochure with your class.

GLOSSARY OF KEY VOCABULARY

Words that are part of the Academic Word List are noted with an **A** in this glossary.

UNIT 1 PEOPLE

READING 1

city (n) a large town

country (n) an area of land that has its own government

date of birth (n) the day you were born

hobby (n) an activity that you enjoy and do regularly

job **A** (n) the work you do to get money

language (n) a type of communication used by the people of a particular country

READING 2

family (n) a group of people related to each other, such as a mother, a father, and their children

interested in (adj phr) wanting to learn more about something

live (v) to have your home somewhere

music (n) sounds that are made by playing instruments or singing

normal **A** (adj) usual, ordinary, and expected

unusual (adj) different and not usual, often in a way that is interesting or exciting

watch (v) to look at something for some time

work (v) to do a job, especially the job you do to get money

UNIT 2 CLIMATE

READING 1

cold (adj) having a low temperature

fall (n) the season of the year between summer and winter when the leaves change color and fall from trees

spring (n) the season of the year between winter and summer, when the plants and trees begin to grow

summer (n) the season of the year when the weather is the warmest

warm (adj) a temperature between cool and hot

winter (n) the season of the year when the weather is the coldest

READING 2

climate (n) the weather that a place usually has

cloudy (adj) with a lot of clouds

dry (adj) with very little or no rain or water

rainfall (n) the amount of rain that falls in one place

rainy (adj) with a lot of rain

season (n) one of the four periods of the year: winter, spring, summer, or fall

sunny (adj) with a lot of sun

windy (adj) with a lot of wind

UNIT 3 LIFESTYLE

READING 1

breakfast (n) the food you eat in the morning after you wake up

cook (v) to prepare food by heating it

dinner (n) the food you eat at the end of the day

get up (phr v) to rise from bed after sleeping

lunch (n) the food you eat in the middle of the day

meet (v) to see and speak to someone for the first time

swim (v) to move through water by moving your body

travel (v) to go from one place to another, usually over a long distance

READING 2

afternoon (n) the period of time between 12:00 p.m. and 5 p.m.

busy (adj) having a lot of things to do

evening (n) the period of time between 5:00 p.m. and 11:00 p.m.

morning (n) the period of time between 5:00 a.m. and 12:00 p.m.

relax Ⓐ (v) to become calm and comfortable

schedule Ⓐ (n) a list of planned activities or things that need to be done

weekday (n) Monday to Friday, when many people work

weekend (n) Saturday and Sunday, when many people do not work

UNIT 4 PLACES

READING 1

forest (n) a large area of trees growing closely together, such as the redwood forest in California

lake (n) a large area of fresh water that has land all around it, such as Lake Michigan

map (n) a picture that shows a place and the rivers, lakes, and other areas in it

mountain (n) a very high hill, such as Mount Everest

ocean (n) one of the five main areas of salt water on Earth, such as the Atlantic and Pacific

river (n) water that flows across the land to a bigger area of water, such as the Mississippi River

sea (n) a large area of salt water, such as the Mediterranean Sea

READING 2

beach (n) an area of sand or rocks next to a sea, ocean, or lake

capital (n) the most important city in a country, where the government is, such as Washington, D.C.

famous (adj) known by many people

international (adj) relating to or involving two or more countries

island (n) land with water all around it

modern (adj) made with new ideas and designs

popular (adj) liked by many people

tourist (n) a person who travels and visits places for fun

UNIT 5 JOBS

READING 1

friendly (adj) nice and kind

healthy (adj) being well; not sick

hospital (n) a place where people who are sick or hurt go for help

in shape (adj) in good health; strong

medicine (n) something you take to feel better

nurse (n) a person who helps doctors and takes care of people

pay (n) the money you receive for doing a job

pilot (n) a person who flies an airplane

READING 2

center (n) a place with a special purpose

company (n) an organization that sells something to make money

engineer (n) a person who designs and builds things

good at (adj) able to do something well

great (adj) very good; excellent

high school (n) a school for children about 15 to 18 years old, between middle school and college or university

interesting (adj) getting your attention because it is exciting; not boring

teacher (n) a person who helps others learn

UNIT 6 HOMES AND BUILDINGS

READING 1

garden (n) an area around a house with grass, flowers, or trees

glass (n) a hard, clear material that windows and bottles are made of

plastic (n) a material that is used in a lot of different ways, e.g. bags, toys, and cups

roof (n) the outside top of a building or vehicle

tall (adj) having a greater than normal height

wall (n) one of the sides of a room or building

window (n) part of a wall that has glass in it, for letting in light and for looking through

wood (n) the hard material that trees are made of

READING 2

apartment (n) a set of rooms for someone to live in on one level of a building or house

building (n) a house, school, office, or store with a roof and walls

cheap (adj) costing little money; not expensive

cost (v) to have an amount of money as a price that someone must pay

elevator (n) a machine, like a small room, that carries people up or down in a tall building

expensive (adj) costing a lot of money; not cheap

UNIT 7 FOOD AND CULTURE

READING 1

bread (n) a basic food made from flour, water, and salt mixed together and baked

different (adj) not like other things

drink (n) a liquid that you drink, for example, water or soda

honey (n) a sweet and sticky food made by bees

prepare (v) to make something

same (adj) like something else

type (n) something that is part of a group of things that are like each other

READING 2

dish (n) food that is prepared in a particular way

fish (n) an animal that lives in water and swims

meal (n) the food that you eat in the morning, afternoon, or evening (breakfast, lunch, and dinner)

meat (n) soft parts of animals, used as food

rice (n) small grains from a plant that are cooked and eaten

serve with (phr v) to give one type of food with another type of food

vegetable (n) plants used as food, such as carrots or spinach

UNIT 8 TRANSPORTATION

READING 1

bike (n) a type of transportation with two wheels that you sit on and move by turning two pedals (= parts you press with your feet); a bicycle

bus (n) a big type of car that takes many people around a city

motorcycle (n) a big bike with an engine for one or two people

subway (n) trains that travel underground, usually in a city

taxi (n) a car with a driver who you pay to take you somewhere

traffic (n) the cars, trucks, etc., driving on the road

train (n) a long, thin type of car that travels on tracks with people or things

transportation Ⓐ (n) the things people use to move themselves or things from one place to another, such as cars, buses, and trains

READING 2

drive (v) to make a car, bus, or train move by controlling it

prefer (v) to like someone or something more than another person or thing

report (n) information about an event or situation

result (n) information that you get from something, like an exam, a survey, a medical test, etc.

ride (v) to travel by sitting in a car or train or on a bike

spend (v) to use time by doing something

take (v) to travel somewhere using a car, bus, or train

VIDEO SCRIPTS

UNIT 1

▶ Thai Fishermen

Narrator: This is Goon, and this is where he lives.

He lives in a village by the sea, on an island called Ko Surin. His island is near the west coast of Thailand in Asia.

Goon and his friends are part of the Moken people. They live on land, but they spend a lot of their time in and on the sea.

The Moken people are very good at sailing, fishing, and diving. But they don't use special equipment or goggles.

They jump from their boat into the water. These boys are very good swimmers. But how can they see to find food underwater without goggles? Goon and his friends are special.

They can see everything underwater easily. Goon can see the beautiful fish and plants around him.

This helps him catch fish and other sea animals for his friends and family.

UNIT 2

▶ The Growing Ice Cap

Narrator: In the beginning of winter here, the days grow short and cold. Snow and cold temperatures move south into parts of North America, Europe, and Asia.

Winter is hard here. Water in the air, in rivers, and in plants turns to ice. As a result, most of the plants die. But some trees, like fir trees and pine trees, can live in very cold temperatures. These trees make up the greatest forest on Earth, called the taiga.

The taiga forest goes around the northern part of the Earth. From Alaska to Canada, from Scandinavia to Russia, it has almost 30% of all the trees on Earth!

During the winter, in the most northern part of the taiga forest, freezing air from the north meets warm air from the south. Heavy snow covers this area of the taiga until warmer temperatures return in the spring.

UNIT 3

▶ Panama's Kuna People

Narrator: The Kuna people live in Colombia and Panama. Almost 35,000 of them live on islands near the coast of Panama called Kuna Yala. They are people of the sea.

Many of the Kuna are fishermen. They sometimes swim more than 100 feet deep and stay underwater for two minutes at a time. They catch fish and lobsters for food.

They also get food from their islands. They grow coconuts on many of the smaller islands. Most of the people live in villages on the larger islands. They have a rich culture, and they wear colorful traditional clothes every day.

The Kuna always take care of their islands and keep their villages clean. Every morning they go to the beach and sweep the sand.

They have small gardens around their homes, and they water their plants every day. They also raise animals.

Music is important to the Kuna men, women, and children. In their free time, they often play music and dance. Their daily life is probably very different from yours and mine.

UNIT 4

▶ The Cenotes of Mexico

Narrator: In the southeast part of Mexico, known as the Yucatán, there are many rich, green forests.

Here, these amazing holes are the only spaces in the trees. They are very deep, they are made of rock, and they are often full of water. Mexicans call these places *cenotes*.

Olmo Torres-Talamante is a scientist. For him, the *cenotes* are very special. He studies them, and the plants and animals in and around them.

Water is very important in the Yucatán. It rains a lot here, but there are no lakes or rivers. When it rains, the water goes down into the rock under the Yucatán. Over time, it makes the *cenotes*.

Cenotes are the only places to find fresh water in the Yucatán. They help the animals and plants in the forest live.

Lily pads, fish, and turtles all live at the top of the *cenotes*, where it's warm and light.

But when Olmo swims deeper into the cave, it gets cold and dark. How can anything live here?

But even here, the scientist finds life.

UNIT 5

▶ Utah's Bingham Mine

Narrator: This is the Bingham copper mine in Utah, in the western United States. It's the largest mine of its kind in the world. And it gets bigger all the time. Today it's two-and-a-half miles wide and almost one mile deep.

Matt Lengerich is the operations manager of the mine.

It produces enough copper each year to make wires for every home in the USA and Mexico. We use copper everywhere—in our homes, cell phones, and cars—and some of it comes from here.

But the rocks contain only a small amount of copper. So Matt's workers have to dig up a lot of rocks to get enough copper. That's why Bingham mine is so big.

Matt's workers use these giant trucks to dig up the copper. Sometimes the copper is so deep that they have to dig for seven years to reach it.

Everything about the mine is big. These giant trucks are heavier than a jumbo jet and work 24 hours a day.

Drivers use the giant trucks to move the rocks and copper.

But they also use something stronger.

The Bingham mine is more than 100 years old, and it's larger than any other mine of its kind.

UNIT 6

▶ To Build the Tallest

Narrator: For almost 4,000 years the Great Pyramid of Egypt was the world's tallest building. It is 455 feet, or almost 140 meters, tall, and it is made of stone.

Then in the year 1311, a small town in Britain finally built something taller.

The Lincoln Cathedral was also made of stone, but its makers used new ways to build it taller. With the three tall spires on top, Lincoln Cathedral was 46 feet, or 14 meters, taller than the Great Pyramid.

To build taller than the pyramids and cathedrals, we needed a new material: steel. In 1887, the Eiffel Tower in Paris, France, became almost two times taller than the Lincoln Cathedral.

In 1930, the Chrysler Building in New York City, used steel to make it the tallest skyscraper in the world.

One year later, the Empire State Building used steel to go even higher.

The next big change was in 1972 when New York's very tall World Trade Center was finished.

One year later, the Sears Tower in Chicago, Illinois, opened. Steel and glass made these buildings light.

Later, the Petronas Towers in Kuala Lumpur, Malaysia, used steel, glass, and concrete.

At 1,667 feet tall, Taipei 101 in Taipei City was the first building to be half a kilometer high. And buildings like the Burj Khalifa in Dubai, in the United Arab Emirates, keep pushing higher.

UNIT 7

▶ Goat Cheese

Narrator: This is the village of Arreau in the south of France. Every Thursday morning in Arreau, there is a market. Here, farmers sell fruit, vegetables, bread, meat, and cheese.

Cheese is very popular in France. And Arreau has some very special cheese—goat cheese.

Mrs. Tuchan sells goat cheese from her farm. Her farm is in a village near Arreau. People can visit the farm to learn how she and her husband make cheese.

First they have to get the milk from the goats. The goats wait at the door. They go into the milking room one by one. Mrs. Tuchan uses a machine to get the milk. She does this twice a day. Each goat can give more than two quarts of milk every day.

Next, the milk goes to a different room – the cheese-making room.

Now they have to turn the milk into cheese. Mr. Tuchan adds an ingredient to the goat milk. Then, he puts it in small plastic cups with holes in the bottom.

The next day, he turns the cheese over. Then he adds some salt to it.

Next, he moves the cheese to another room. The cheese stays here for one to three weeks. Then it will be ready to sell, and to eat.

UNIT 8

▶ Modern Subways

Narrator: How do people in big cities travel? Many of them take the subway. Subways move millions of people underground every day. There are over 150 subway systems in the world today.

The oldest one is in London, England.

There, everyone calls it the "Tube."

At 8:00 a.m., the Tube really gets busy. In the morning, over 500,000 Londoners go to work by subway. Of course, people on the streets can't see them.

But what if the Tube ran above the ground?

Every day in London, over 500 trains on 250 miles of track move nearly 3 million people.

That's a lot of people, but the busiest subway system in the world is in Tokyo, Japan.

There are more people in Tokyo than in any other city in the world. Around 35,000 people take the Tokyo subway every hour. That means 8 million riders travel underground every day.

On every platform, there are 25 subway attendants, like Yuhei Mitsuhashi.

They keep the riders safe, calm, and on time, because the trains cannot be late.

CREDITS

The authors and publishers acknowledge the following sources of copyright material and are grateful for the permissions granted. While every effort has been made, it has not always been possible to identify the sources of all the material used, or to trace all copyright holders. If any omissions are brought to our notice, we will be happy to include the appropriate acknowledgements on reprinting and in the next update to the digital edition, as applicable.

Photo credits

Key: T = Top, C = Center, B = Below, L = Left, R = Right, TL = Top Left, TR = Top Right, BL = Below Left, BR = Below Right, CL = Center Left, CR = Center Right, BG = Background.

p. 12: Cultura RM Exclusive/Peter Muller/Getty Images; pp. 14–15: Mitchell Funk/Getty Images; p. 19: Scott Halleran/Getty Images Sport/Getty Images; p. 22 (T): Bernd Thissen/DPA/Getty Images; p. 22 (B): Mac99/iStock/Getty Images; p. 29 (TR): Image Source/Getty Images; p. 29 (BL): Takayuki/Shutterstock; p. 34 (photo a): Juanmonino/iStock/Getty Images; p. 34 (photo b): Absodels/Getty Images; p. 34 (photo c): Topic Images Inc./Getty Images; pp. 36–37: Francesco Iacobelli/AWL Images/Getty Images; p. 41 (skating): noblige/iStock/Getty Images; p. 41 (skiing): wojciech_gajda/iStock/Getty Images; p. 41 (BL): Bill Bachmann/First Light/Getty Images; p. 44: Kamira/Shutterstock; pp. 52–53: wellsie82/Moment/Getty Images; pp. 58–59: Lonely Planet/Getty Images; p. 63 (T, BL): John Noble/Lonely Planet Images/Getty Images; p. 63 (BR): Johnny Haglund/Lonely Planet Images/Getty Images; pp. 80–81: Michele Falzone/AWL Images/Getty Images; p. 85: UniversalImagesGroup/Getty Images; p. 88 (L): Photogerson/Shutterstock; p. 88 (R): Buena Vista Images/Photodisc/Getty Images; pp. 102–103: Reza/Getty Images News/Getty Images; pp. 124–125: JaCZhou 2015/Moment Open/Getty Images; p. 128 (window): Blair_witch/iStock/Getty Images; p. 128 (roof): kcconsulting/iStock/Getty Images; p. 128 (cups): schantalao/iStock/Getty Images; p. 128 (garden): S.B. Nace/Lonely Planet Images/Getty Images; p. 128 (girl): Jamie Grill/Iconica/Getty Images; p. 128 (buildings): FUTURE LIGHT/Photolibrary/Getty Images; p. 128 (glass): Peter Starman/Getty Images; p. 128 (table): Zsolt Bute/EyeEm/Getty Images; p. 129 (architect): Jetta Productions/Iconica/Getty Images; p. 129 (CL): View Pictures/Universal Images Group/Getty Images; p. 129 (C): Deconphotostudio; p. 129 (CR): Architecture: Lada Hrsak and Danielle Huls, photography ©Thomas Landen; p. 132 (L): gionnixxx/iStock/Getty Images; p. 132 (C): Gavin Hellier/AWL Images/Getty Images; p. 132 (R): Ed Norton/Lonely Planet Images/Getty Images; p. 134: George Rose/Getty Images News/Getty Images; pp. 146–147: Steve Vidler/Alamy; p. 151 (TL): Carlina Teteris/Moment/Getty Images; p. 151 (BR): Danita Delimont/Gallo Images/Getty Images; p. 151 (BL): Gaza Press/REX/Shutterstock; p. 153 (photo a): Antonio Ciufo/Moment Open/Getty Images; p. 153 (photo b): James Smedley/First Light/Getty Images; p. 153 (photo c): ed073/iStock/Getty Images; p. 153 (photo d): Bridget Davey/Moment Mobile/Getty Images; p. 153 (photo e): Julia Sudnitskaya/iStock/Getty Images; p. 153 (photo f): Kelvin Kam/EyeEm/Getty Images; p. 153 (photo g): Jennifer Levy/StockFood Creative/Getty Images; p. 154 (T): Hisham Ibrahim/Moment Mobile/Getty Images; p. 154 (C): Amateur photographer, still learning/Moment Open/Getty Images; p. 154 (B): Martin Robinson/Lonely Planet Images/Getty Images; p. 163: RunPhoto/The Image Bank/Getty Images; pp. 168–169: Thanapol Marattana/Moment/Getty Images; p. 173 (L): Will Gray/AWL Images/Getty Images; p. 173 (C): AaronChenPs/Moment/Getty Images; p. 173 (R): Joel Carillet/E+/Getty Images; p. 176: Universal Images Group/Getty Images; p. 178: Amit Goldstein/EyeEm/Getty Images; p. 188 (photo a): DMEPhotography/iStock/Getty Images; p. 188 (photo b): Daniel Ernst/iStock/Getty Images; p. 188 (photo c): ArabianEye/Getty Images.

Front cover photographs by (girl) BestPhotoStudio/Shutterstock and (BG) Andrei Medvedev/Shutterstock.

Illustrations

by Martin Sanders (Beehive Illustration) p. 88; Rudolf Farkas (Beehive Illustration) p. 91.

Video Supplied by BBC Worldwide Learning.

Video Stills Supplied by BBC Worldwide Learning.

Corpus

Development of this publication has made use of the Cambridge English Corpus (CEC). The CEC is a multi-billion word computer database of contemporary spoken and written English. It includes British English, American English, and other varieties of English. It also includes the Cambridge Learner Corpus, developed in collaboration with the University of Cambridge ESOL Examinations. Cambridge University Press has built up the CEC to provide evidence about language use that helps to produce better language teaching materials.

Cambridge Dictionaries

Cambridge dictionaries are the world's most widely used dictionaries for learners of English. The dictionaries are available in print and online at dictionary.cambridge.org. Copyright © Cambridge University Press, reproduced with permission.

Typeset by emc design ltd.

INFORMED BY TEACHERS

Classroom teachers shaped everything about *Prism*. The topics. The exercises. The critical thinking skills. The On Campus sections. Everything. We are confident that *Prism* will help your students succeed in college because teachers just like you helped guide the creation of this series.

Prism Advisory Panel

The members of the *Prism* Advisory Panel provided inspiration, ideas, and feedback on many aspects of the series. *Prism* is stronger because of their contributions.

Gloria Munson
University of Texas, Arlington

Dinorah Sapp
University of Mississippi

Kim Oliver
Austin Community College

Christine Hagan
George Brown College/Seneca College

Gregory Wayne
Portland State University

Heidi Lieb
Bergen Community College

Julaine Rosner
Mission College

Stephanie Kasuboski
Cuyahoga Community College

Global Input

Teachers from more than 500 institutions all over the world provided valuable input through:
- Surveys
- Focus Groups
- Reviews